JANICE VANCLEAVE'S

Help! My Science Project Is Due Tomorrow!

Easy Experiments You Can Do Overnight

JOSSEY-BASS
A Wiley Imprint
www.josseybass.com

Published by Jossey-Bass
A Wiley Imprint
989 Market Street, San Francisco, CA 94103-1741   www.josseybass.com

Published simultaneously in Canada

Design and production by Navta Associates, Inc.

The publisher and the author have made every reasonable effort to insure that the experiments and activities in the book are safe when conducted as instructed but assume no responsibility for any damage caused or sustained while performing the experiments or activities in this book. Parents, guardians, and/or teachers should supervise young readers who undertake the experiments and activities in this book.

Readers should be aware that Internet Web sites offered as citations and/or sources for further information may have changed or disappeared between the time this was written and when it is read.

Jossey-Bass books and products are available through most bookstores. To contact Jossey-Bass directly call our Customer Care Department within the U.S. at 800-956-7739, outside the U.S. at 317-572-3986, or fax 317-572-4002.

Jossey-Bass also publishes its books in a variety of electronic formats. Some content that appears in print may not be available in electronic books.

Library of Congress Cataloging-in-Publication Data

VanCleave, Janice Pratt.
    [Help! my science project is due tomorrow!]
    Janice VanCleave's help! my science project is due tomorrow! : easy experiments you can do overnight.
        p. cm.
    Includes bibliographical references and index.
    ISBN 0-471-33100-7 (pbk. : acid-free paper)
    1. Science projects—Juvenile literature. [1. Science projects.] I. Title: Help! my science project is due tomorrow!. II. Title.

Q182.3 . V353 2001
507'.8—dc21   2001026253

Printed in the United States of America
FIRST EDITION
PB Printing   10 9 8

Dedication

This book is dedicated to a very knowledgeable and talented teacher, whose help in writing this book was invaluable. What a pleasure it has been to work with my friend and colleague, Holly Harris.

I wish to express my appreciation to these science specialists for their valuable assistance by providing information or assisting me in finding it.

Members of the Central Texas Astronomical Society, including Johnny Barton, John W. McAnally, and Paul Derrick. Johnny is an officer of the society and has been an active amateur astronomer for more than 20 years. John is on the staff of the Association of Lunar and Planetary Observers where he is acting Assistant Coordinator for Transit Timings of the Jupiter Section. Paul is the author of the "Stargazer" column in the *Waco Tribune-Herald.*

Dr. Glenn S. Orton, a Senior Research Scientist at the Jet Propulsion Laboratory of the California Institute of Technology. Glenn is an astronomer and space scientist who specializes in investigating the structure and composition of planetary atmospheres. He is best known for his research on Jupiter and Saturn. I have enjoyed exchanging ideas with Glenn about experiments for modeling astronomy experiments.

Dr. Laura Barge, Senior Research Fellow, CASPER (Center for Astrophysics, Space Physics & Engineering Research). Dr. Ben Doughty, head of the department of physics at Texas A & M University—Commerce in Commerce, Texas. Laura and Ben have helped me to better understand the fun of learning about physics.

Robert Fanick, a chemist at Southwest Research Institute in San Antonio, Texas, and Virginia Malone, a science assessment consultant. These two very special people have provided a great deal of valuable information, which has made this book even more understandable and fun.

Marsha Willis, Middle School Science Coordinator at Region 12 Educational Center, Waco, Texas. Marsha has not only assisted with reviewing the activities for this book but was instrumental in our being involved in NASA's Texas Fly High Program, which provided the opportunity for me to fly in NASA's KC-135A zero-g aircraft, commonly called the Vomit Comet.

A special note of gratitude to these educators who assisted by pretesting the activities and/or by providing scientific information: Laura Roberts, St. Matthews Elementary, Louisville, Kentucky.

Contents

Introduction — 1

Astronomy — 3

1. Lineup (Solar System) — 4
2. Night Sky (Sky Measurement) — 6
3. Star Clock (Star Distances) — 8
4. Coverup (Eclipses) — 10
5. Sun Path (Sun) — 12
6. Escape (Satellites) — 14
7. Morning Star (Venus) — 16
8. Splat! (Meteorites) — 18
9. Fill 'Er Up (Telescopes) — 20
10. Moon Phase (Moon) — 22

Biology — 25

11. Building Blocks (Cells) — 26
12. Patterns (Leaves) — 28
13. Water Loss (Transpiration) — 30
14. In and Out (Osmosis) — 32
15. Snares (Spiders) — 34
16. Identify (Fingerprints) — 36
17. Foamy (Microbes) — 38
18. Oops! (Reaction Time) — 40
19. Tasty (Taste) — 42
20. Inhale, Exhale (Lung Capacity) — 44

Chemistry — 47

21. Changes (Phases of Matter) — 48
22. New Stuff (Chemical Changes) — 50
23. Glob (Polymers) — 52
24. Soakers (Absorption) — 54
25. Riser (Specific Gravity) — 56
26. Mixers (Solutions) — 58
27. Separator (Chromatography) — 60
28. Meltdown! (Ice) — 62
29. Cleanup! (Emulsifiers) — 64
30. Brown Banana (Oxidation) — 66

Earth Science — 69

31. Wet or Dry? (Humidity) — 70
32. How Fast? (Wind) — 72
33. Fluffy (Snow) — 74
34. Warmup (Temperature) — 76
35. Around and Around (Water Cycle) — 78
36. Airy (Soil) — 80
37. Washout (Erosion) — 82
38. Settling (Settling Rate) — 84
39. Squirter (Water Pressure) — 86
40. Overflow (Rocks) — 88

Physics — 91

41. Equal (Potential Energy) — 92
42. Spreader (Diffraction) — 94
43. Pickup! (Static Electricity) — 96
44. Swingers (Pendulums) — 98
45. Spinners (Inertia) — 100
46. Spacey (Matter) — 102
47. Trapped (Insulators) — 104
48. Sliders (Heat) — 106
49. Stretchy (Elasticity) — 108
50. High or Low? (Sound) — 110

Glossary — 113

Index — 117

Introduction

So you want to do a science project. Great! You'll get to show off your work to your class and you may even get an award. But the best part is that you'll learn a lot about science by observing, investigating, and sharing what you have learned with others. I hope that you haven't really left your science project until the last minute, because you'll get a lot more out of your project (and probably get a better grade) if you take your time. You can do the exploratory investigations in this book overnight, but I hope that you'll consider working on the extensions, doing research, and using what you've discovered from the investigation to come up with your own great science project.

A science project is like a mystery in which you are the detective searching for answers. But with a science project, you get to select which mystery to solve. After you've selected your mystery, you can creatively design methods to uncover clues. These clues eventually should lead to the final revelation of who, what, when, where, how, and why.

This book presents fun project ideas on a wide variety of subjects from astronomy, biology, chemistry, earth science, and physics. In the 50 chapters, you'll find investigations, facts, ideas, and questions for projects you can do easily all on your own. It's your job to pick a topic, discover the answers, and develop the ideas into a terrific project!

How to Use This Book

You can start anywhere in the book. Flip through the chapters for a topic that sounds interesting. Before you do any of the investigations, read the chapter through completely. Once you've decided on a project, collect all the materials needed for the investigation and follow procedures carefully. The format for each chapter is as follows:

- **So You Want to Do a Project about . . .** A statement introducing the topic of the project
- **Let's Explore** An exploratory investigation that will become part of your research
- **Purpose** A statement of the investigation's objective
- **Materials** A complete list of what you'll need
- **Procedure** A step-by-step walk-through that shows you how to do the investigation
- **Results** A statement of the expected outcome
- **Why?** An explanation of why the investigation works. When a new term is introduced and explained, it appears in **bold** type; these terms can also be found in the Glossary.
- **For Further Investigation** An example of the way the data from the investigation can be used to develop a project question on the same topic
- **Clues for Your Investigation** Ideas for ways to experimentally answer the project question. Some chapters include special ideas for displaying your science project.
- **Other Questions to Explore** A list of other possible science questions for you to think about in creating your own projects
- **References and Project Books** A list of books where information and other project ideas about the topic presented in the chapter can be found. It is important to get information from many different sources so that you will be as informed as possible. You can use Internet search engines if these resources are approved by your parent and teacher. No Web site URLs are listed in this book because of the possibility of sites being canceled or having a change of address.

General Instructions for the Projects

1. Read the investigations completely before starting.
2. Collect supplies. You will have less frustration and more fun if all the materials necessary for the investigation are ready before you start. You lose your train of thought when you have to stop and search for supplies. Ask an adult for advice before substituting any materials.
3. Do not rush. Follow each step very carefully; never skip steps, and do not add your own. Safety is of the utmost importance. By reading each investigation before starting, then following the instructions exactly, you can feel confident that no unexpected results will occur.
4. Observe. If your results are not the same as those described in the investigation, carefully reread the instructions and start over from step 1.

General Display Tips

You may be asked to display your project. A project display represents all the work that you have done. It should consist of a backboard, and anything that represents your project, such as models, photographs, graphs of results, and the like. It must tell the story of the project in such a way that it attracts and holds the interest of the viewer. It has to be thorough, but not too crowded, so keep it simple and neat.

You may wish to purchase a display backboard at a local teaching supply or business supply store. Or you can make a three-sided backboard from sturdy cardboard with duct tape to secure the panels together.

The title and other headings should be neat and large enough to be read at a distance of about 3 feet (1 m). You can buy precut stick-on letters for the title and heading, or you can cut your own letters out of construction paper and glue them on. You can also stencil the letters for all the titles directly on the backboard. Another option is to use a word processor or computer to print the title and headings.

Your teacher may have set rules for the position of the information as well as the different headings. These headings may include

- **Problem**   The project question
- **Hypothesis**   An idea about the solution to a problem, based on knowledge and research
- **Procedure**   The steps of the project experiment
- **Data**   Your observations presented in tables and graphs
- **Results**   A summary of the data
- **Conclusion**   A summary of the results of your project investigation and a statement of how the results compare to the hypothesis

Astronomy

1 Lineup

So You Want to Do a Project about the **Solar System!**

LET'S EXPLORE

Purpose

To make a model of what scientists in the past thought the universe looked like.

Materials

    drawing compass
    ruler
    16-inch (40-cm) -square piece of white poster board
    scissors
    7 different colored crayons—1 each of blue, yellow, red, and 4 other colors
    strip of adding machine paper (length of the clothes hanger)
    transparent tape
    marking pen
    clothes hanger
    48-inch (120-cm) piece of string

Procedure

1. Use the compass to draw sixteen 1½-inch (3.75-cm) -diameter circles on the poster board.
2. Cut out the circles. You should have 16 circles.
3. Using the blue crayon, color the front and back of two of the circles.
4. Make a slit from the circumference to the center point of each of the two colored circles.
5. Take the two colored circles and join them together at the slits at right angles to model a 3-D sphere.
6. Repeat steps 3 to 5 using the remaining crayons and circles.
7. Repeat step 5 with the two remaining, uncolored circles.
8. Fold the adding machine paper in half three times. Unfold the strip of paper and

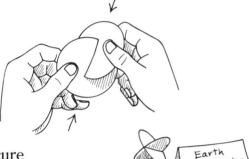

Earth
1 cm = 3,000 km

    secure it to the clothes hanger with tape.

9. Use the pen to label the parts of the universe on the paper strip, starting with Earth at the left end, in this order: Earth, Moon, Mercury, Venus, Sun, Mars, Jupiter, and Saturn. Put all the labels except "Earth" on the fold lines as shown.
10. Cut the string into eight equal pieces, each 6 inches (15 cm) long.
11. Tape one end of each piece of string to the top of each model sphere. Attach the free ends of the strings to the hanger. Each sphere represents one celestial body. Tape the blue sphere to the hanger at the Earth label, the white sphere at the Moon label, yellow at the Sun label, and red at the Mars label. The other colored spheres can be attached to represent any planet.
12. Hold the Earth end of the hanger in place and rotate the hanger around once. Observe the motion of the celestial bodies.

Results

You have made a model that shows how scientists in the past thought the universe was organized. The celestial bodies moved around Earth.

Why?

In this investigation, you have made a **geocentric** (Earth-centered) model of the

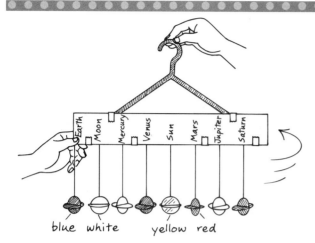

blue white   yellow red

universe (Earth and all natural objects in space regarded as a whole). Ptolemy and most scientists of the second century A.D. believed that Earth was motionless and all **celestial bodies** (natural objects in the sky, such as moons, planets, suns, and stars) **revolved** (moved in a curved path around another object) around Earth. An outer dome of stars was thought to exist beyond the farthest planet (then thought to be Saturn). Ptolemy believed that in relation to their starry background, the Sun and the Moon moved along regular paths around Earth, while other celestial bodies seemed to wander. These wandering celestial bodies were called **planets** from the Greek word for *wanderers.* (Planets today are known to be celestial bodies that revolve about the Sun.) The curved path of one celestial body about another is called an **orbit.** Orbited and revolved both mean to move in such a path.

In 1543, the Polish astronomer Nicolaus Copernicus (1473–1543) proposed a **heliocentric** (Sun-centered) model of the universe. Copernicus was not the first to suggest that the Sun was the center of the universe, but he was the first to propose a model that at the time best explained the movement of the celestial bodies.

FOR FURTHER INVESTIGATION

Although Copernicus and Ptolemy believed their models represented the entire universe, they mainly attempted to explain the relationship between objects in our **solar system** (a group of celestial bodies that orbits a star is

called a sun). A project question might be, How does Copernicus's model of the universe compare with the modern model of our solar system?

Clues for Your Investigation

1. Research and find out about Copernicus's model as well as the modern model of our solar system.
2. Use the materials list from the original experiment to prepare representations of Copernicus's model of the universe and the modern model of the solar system. Display the ancient and modern models and describe the differences between them.

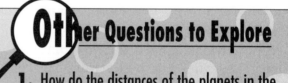

Other Questions to Explore

1. How do the distances of the planets in the solar system compare?
2. How do the sizes of the planets in the solar system compare?

REFERENCES AND PROJECT BOOKS

Asimov, Isaac. *Astronomy Projects.* Milwaukee: Gareth Stevens, 1996.

Couper, Heather, and Nigel Henbest. *How the Universe Works.* Pleasantville, N.Y.: Reader's Digest, 1994.

Nicolson, Cynthia Pratt. *The Planets.* Toronto: Kids Can Press, 1998.

Pasachoff, Jay M. *Peterson First Guides: Solar System.* Boston: Houghton Mifflin, 1995.

Paul, Richard. *A Handbook to the Universe.* Chicago: Chicago Review Press, 1993.

VanCleave, Janice. *Janice VanCleave's A+ Projects in Astronomy.* New York: Wiley, 2001.

———. *Janice VanCleave's Astronomy for Every Kid.* New York: Wiley, 1991.

———. *Janice VanCleave's Solar System.* New York: Wiley, 2000.

Walker, Jane. *The Solar System.* Brookfield, Conn.: Millbrook Press, 1994.

Wood, Robert W. *Science for Kids: 39 Easy Astronomy Experiments.* Blue Ridge Summit, Pa.: Tab Books, 1991.

LET'S EXPLORE

Purpose

To use your hands to measure sky distances.

Materials

your hands

Procedure

1. Stand outdoors in a clear area so that the horizon, where the sky appears to touch Earth, is visible.
2. Measure the distance from the point directly overhead to the horizon. Do this using the following steps:

   - Make a fist with one hand and hold this hand at arm's length over your head.

- Make a fist with your other hand and put this fist under the first as shown.

- Keeping your arms extended, lower your fists to the horizon by moving one fist under the other, counting each one until the bottom of one fist appears to touch the horizon. How many fists did you use?

Results

Nine fists are generally needed to make the measurement.

Why?

You used your hands to measure the angular distance from the **zenith** (the point directly overhead) to the **horizon** (an imaginary line where the sky seems to meet Earth). **Angular distance** is the apparent or observed distance between distant objects, usually measured in degrees. For measuring angular distances in the sky, the width of a person's fist held at arm's length measures about 10°. A person with longer arms generally has wider hands, so generally everyone's fist measures an angular distance of 10°. Thus, a measurement of nine fists from the zenith to the horizon is an angular measurement of 90°.

FOR FURTHER INVESTIGATION

Other parts of the hand can be used to measure larger or smaller angular distances, such as distances between stars. Do the distances between stars in a **constellation** (a group of stars that form a pattern in the sky) change? A project question might be, How do the distances between the stars in the **Big Dipper** (part of the Ursa Major Constellation) compare from one hour to the next during the night?

Clues for Your Investigation

1. On a clear, moonless night, and as early in the evening as possible, use the hand measurements shown here to measure the angular distance between the end stars of the Big Dipper or between any two stars. Decide on a consistent method of measuring. For example, you may wish to measure the distance between the centers of the stars, as shown here.

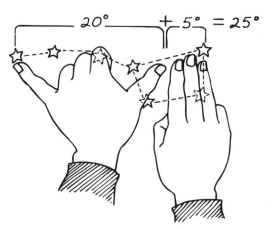

2. Repeat the measurement every hour for 3 or more hours.
3. For the most accurate results, make four or more measurements, recording them in an Angular Distance Data table like the one shown. Average the measurements for each observation time and compare them.
4. You may wish to make a drawing indicating the stars and hand measurements used, similar to the figure shown for clue 1.

ANGULAR DISTANCE DATA

Time	Angular Distance, °				
	Trial 1	Trial 2	Trial 3	Trial 4	Average
8 P.M.					
9 P.M.					
10 P.M.					

Other Questions to Explore

1. What is the angular distance that stars move each hour?
2. What is the change in angular distance of stars from day to day? What causes this change?

REFERENCES AND PROJECT BOOKS

Berry, Richard. *Discover the Stars.* New York: Harmony Books, 1987.

Couper, Heather, and Nigel Henbest. *How the Universe Works.* Pleasantville, N.Y.: Reader's Digest, 1994.

Dickinson, Terence. *Exploring the Night Sky.* Buffalo, N.Y.: Firefly Books, 1987.

Estalella, Robert. *The Stars.* Hauppauge, N.Y.: Barron's, 1993.

Rey, H. A. *The Stars.* Boston: Houghton Mifflin, 1976.

Ridpath, Ian. *Stars and Planets Atlas.* New York: Facts on File, 1997.

VanCleave, Janice. *Janice VanCleave's Constellations for Every Kid.* New York: Wiley, 1997.

———. *Janice VanCleave's Solar System.* New York: Wiley, 2000.

Wood, Robert W. *Science for Kids: 39 Easy Astronomy Experiments.* Blue Ridge Summit, Pa.: Tab Books, 1991.

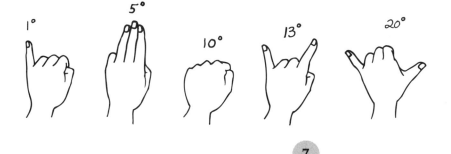

LET'S EXPLORE

Purpose

To determine the daily motion of the Big Dipper.

Materials

drawing compass
12-inch (30-cm) -square piece of poster board
ruler
scissors
pen
pushpin
paper brad

Procedure

1. Use the compass to draw two circles on the poster board, one with a 6-inch (15-cm) and the other with a 5-inch (12.5-cm) diameter. Cut out the circles.
2. Photocopy the Star pattern shown here. Cut out the pattern and glue it to the small circle (star wheel). (The outer time wheel pattern will be used in the following experiment.)
3. Use the pushpin to make a hole through the center of each circle, then assemble the two pieces by putting the star wheel on top of the larger circle (outer wheel) so that the holes in the center line up. *NOTE: The North Star is in the center of the star wheel.*
4. Insert the paper brad through the holes to hold the wheels together.
5. Holding the outer wheel, rotate the star wheel in a counterclockwise direction one full turn. Observe the movement of the Big Dipper in relation to the North Star.

Results

The stars of the Big Dipper move counter-clockwise around the North Star (Polaris).

Why?

The apparent motion of stars results from the **rotation** (turning) of Earth on its **axis** (an imaginary line that passes through the center of an object and around which the object rotates). The daily circular path of stars is called their **diurnal circle.**

FOR FURTHER INVESTIGATION

Since the stars of the Big Dipper appear to move around the North Star each day, they can be used to determine time. A project question might be, How can the movement of the Big Dipper be used to tell time?

Clues for Your Investigation

1. The wheels can be used to construct a star clock.
2. Prepare a time wheel by dividing half of the outer wheel into 12 equal parts. Label the parts from 6 P.M. to 6 A.M. as shown.
3. After dark on a clear night, face north and locate the Big Dipper above the northern horizon.
4. Turn the star wheel until the outline of the Big Dipper lines up with the Big Dipper's position in the sky.
5. Turn the time wheel until the time lines up with the date of the observation.

- Repeat the previous steps, making observations about every hour for 3 or more hours. *NOTE: Compensate for daylight saving time when it is in effect by adding 1 hour.*

Other Questions to Explore

1. What is the relationship between the altitude of Polaris and the latitude of an observer?

2. Because Earth also revolves around the Sun, do stars appear exactly in the same place at the same time each day?

REFERENCES AND PROJECT BOOKS

Baker, Robert H., and Herbert Spencer Zim. *Stars: A Guide to the Constellations, Sun, Moon, Planets, and Other Features of the Heavens.* New York: Golden Press, 1985.

Chartrand, Mark R. *National Audubon Society Field Guide to the Night Sky.* New York: Knopf, 1995.

Couper, Heather, and Nigel Henbest. *How the Universe Works.* Pleasantville, N.Y.: Reader's Digest, 1994.

Harrington, Philip, and Edward Pascuzzi. *Astronomy for All Ages.* Guilford, Conn.: Globe Pequot Press, 1994.

Moché, Dinah L. *Astronomy: A Self-Teaching Guide.* New York: Wiley, 1996.

Moeschl, Richard. *Exploring the Sky.* Chicago: Chicago Review Press, 1993.

Pasachoff, Jay M. *Peterson First Guides: Astronomy.* Boston: Houghton Mifflin, 1997.

VanCleave, Janice. *Janice Van Cleave's Astronomy for Every Kid.* New York: Wiley, 1991.

———. *Janice VanCleave's Constellations for Every Kid.* New York: Wiley, 1997.

Wood, Robert W. *Science for Kids: 39 Easy Astronomy Experiments.* Blue Ridge Summit, Pa.: Tab Books, 1991.

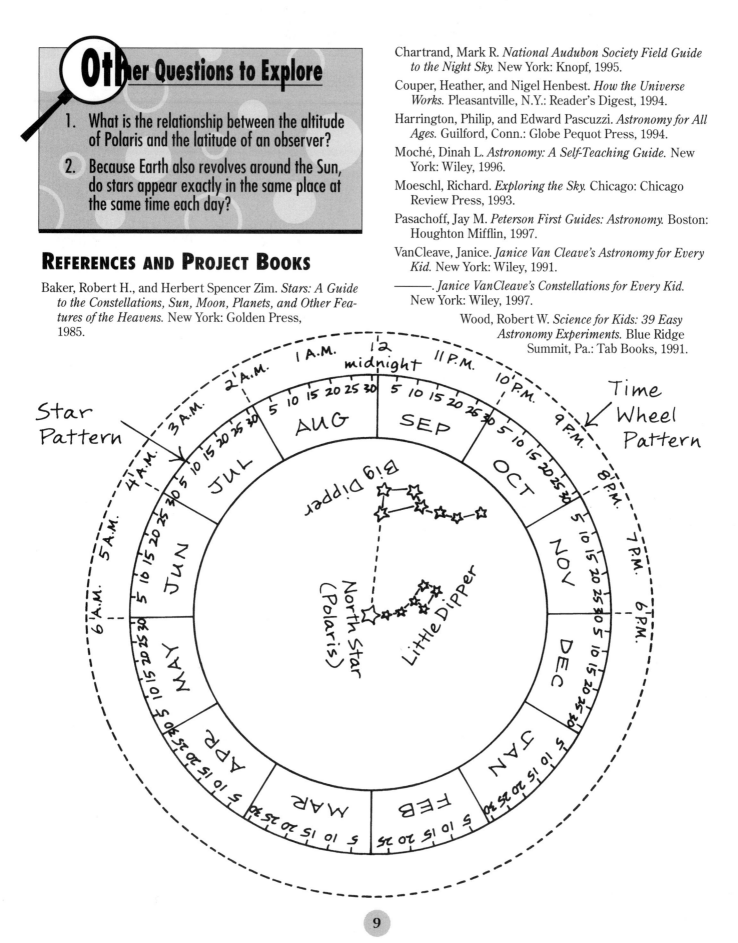

4 Coverup

So You Want to Do a Project about **Eclipses!**

LET'S EXPLORE

Purpose

To demonstrate how the Moon can block your view of the Sun.

Materials

drawing compass
ruler
10-inch (25-cm) -square piece of yellow poster board
scissors
black marker
transparent tape
yardstick (meterstick)
2-inch (5-cm) -square piece of colorless transparent plastic

Procedure

1. Use the drawing compass to draw an 8-inch (20-cm) -diameter circle on the poster board. Draw a 1-by-2-inch (2.5-by-5-cm) tab off one edge of the circle.
2. Cut out the circle and tab. Use the marker to label the circle "Sun."
3. Bend the tab and tape it to the end of a measuring stick so that the circle stands perpendicular to the stick. The paper Sun should be at the end opposite zero on the stick.
4. Lay the measuring stick on a table with the zero end slightly past the edge of the table. Secure the stick with tape.
5. Use the compass to draw a 1-inch (2.5-cm) -diameter circle on the transparent plastic. Cut out the circle. Label it "M" for Moon.
6. Look at the paper Sun at eye level, positioning yourself directly in front of the Sun with the measuring stick touching your cheek below one eye.
7. Hold the Moon circle vertically on the measuring stick.
8. Open the eye above the measuring stick and close the other eye.
9. Move the Moon toward and away from the Sun until a position is found where the Moon appears to be the same size as the Sun.
10. Record the distances of the Sun and Moon from your eye in a distance data table.
11. Calculate the Sun/Moon distance ratio by dividing the Sun's distance by the Moon's distance. For example, if the Sun's distance is 36 inches (90 cm) and the Moon's distance is 9 inches (22.5 cm), the Sun/Moon distance ratio is 36/9 (90/22.5), which reduces to 4/1.

Results

The closer the Moon circle is to your face, the more of the paper Sun it covers. When the

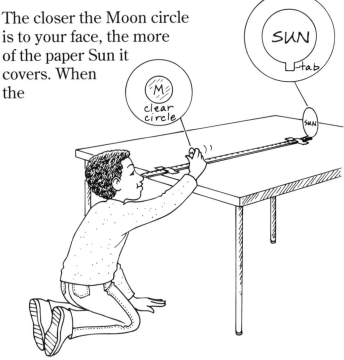

Sun and Moon appear to be the same size, the Sun/Moon distance ratio will be equal to or close to 4/1.

Why?

The closer an object is to your eye, the bigger its **apparent size** (the size an object at a distance appears to be). A smaller circle like the Moon circle can appear to totally cover a larger circle like the paper Sun. In the same way, the Moon, with a diameter of 2,173 miles (3,477 km), can sometimes appear to cover the much larger Sun, which has a diameter of 870,000 miles (1,392,000 km).

When the Moon passes directly between the Sun and Earth and the shadow of the Moon moves across Earth, the Moon is said to **eclipse** (pass in front of and block the light of) the Sun. When the Moon is in this position, observers on Earth see a **solar eclipse.** The Sun is about 400 times larger than the Moon, but at times during the Moon's **elliptical** (oval-shaped) orbit, the Sun is about 400 times farther away from Earth than the Moon. It is in this position that the Moon and Sun appear to be the same size.

In a **total solar eclipse,** the Moon completely blocks the Sun's light from observers on Earth. During a total solar eclipse, the Moon's **umbra** (the darker inner region of a shadow) reaches Earth. The umbra is about 188 miles (300 km) wide and generally moves from west to east. People on Earth in the Moon's umbra see the total solar eclipse, while those in the Moon's **penumbra** (the lighter outer region of a shadow) see only a partial solar eclipse and those outside the penumbra see no eclipse.

FOR FURTHER INVESTIGATION

In a **partial solar eclipse,** only part of the Sun is eclipsed by the Moon. A project question might be, What conditions result in a partial solar eclipse?

Clues for Your Investigation

1. Repeat the original experiment. When the Moon circle is in a position so that it covers the paper Sun, keep the Moon stationary but slowly move your head to the right until the Moon no longer appears to cover any part of the Sun. Make note of the position of the Sun, the Moon, and your open eye (which represents an observer on Earth) during this motion.
2. Your display could include a diagram showing the positions of the Sun, the Moon, and Earth during total and partial solar eclipses, as well as the approximate positions where the Moon's shadow moves across Earth. Label the positions of observers on Earth who would see a total, a partial, or no solar eclipse.

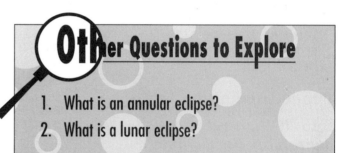

Other Questions to Explore

1. What is an annular eclipse?
2. What is a lunar eclipse?

REFERENCES AND PROJECT BOOKS

Harrington, Philip S. *Eclipse!* New York: Wiley, 1997.

Odenwald, Sten F. *The Astronomy Cafe.* New York: W. H. Freeman, 1998.

Pasachoff, Jay M. *Peterson First Guides: Astronomy.* Boston: Houghton Mifflin, 1997.

Paul, Richard. *A Handbook to the Universe.* Chicago: Chicago Review Press, 1993.

Snowden, Sheila. *The Young Astronomer.* London: Usborne, 1989.

VanCleave, Janice. *Janice VanCleave's Astronomy for Every Kid.* New York: Wiley, 1991.

———. *Janice VanCleave's Solar System.* New York: Wiley, 2000.

Wood, Robert W. *Science for Kids: 39 Easy Astronomy Experiments.* Blue Ridge Summit, Pa.: Tab Books, 1991.

5 Sun Path

So You Want to Do a Project about the **Sun!**

LET'S EXPLORE

Purpose

To model the Sun's shadows at the equator during the equinox.

Materials

5 tablespoons (75 mL) plaster of paris
2 tablespoons (30 mL) tap water
3-ounce (90-mL) paper cup
pencil
white poster board
marker
20-inch (50-cm) string
flashlight
yardstick (meterstick)
protractor
helper

Procedure

CAUTION: Do not wash plaster down the drain. It can clog the drain.

1. Put the plaster of paris and water in the cup. Mix with the pencil.
2. Stand the pencil vertically in the middle of the plaster. Allow the plaster to dry. This may take 30 minutes or more.
3. Lay the poster board on a table and use the marker to label the sides of the poster board "North," "East," "South," and "West."
4. Set the cup of dry plaster in the center of the poster board.
5. Tie one end of the string to the bulb end of the flashlight and the other end to the top of the pencil.
6. In a darkened room, hold the flashlight on the east side of the poster board so that the string is straight and the flashlight is level with the top of the pencil.

7. Ask your helper to measure the shadow cast by the light from the cup to the end of the shadow of the pencil. Record the length as the shadow length for the light at sunrise, 0°, in a Shadow Length Data table like the one shown. Also write a description or make a drawing of the shape of the shadow and indicate its direction.
8. Stand the protractor on top of the pencil so that the protractor faces east. Then, move the flashlight in a circular path stopping above the 90° mark on the protractor, keeping the string straight and the flashlight directed toward the pencil. Repeat step 7. Record this measurement as the shadow length at noontime.

Results

At 0°, the shadow is long and points toward the west. At 90°, there is little or no shadow around the base of the cup.

12

Shadow Length Data

Light Angle	Shadow Length, inches (cm)	Shadow Description
Sunrise, 0°		
Noontime, 90°		

Why?

As Earth rotates, the Sun appears to rise in the morning and travel in an **arc** (segment of a circle) across the sky. This apparent path of the Sun across the sky is called the **ecliptic.**

The **equator** is an imaginary line that circles the center of Earth. In the **Northern Hemisphere** (area north of the equator), the **equinox** is the first day of spring (on or about March 21) or fall (on or about September 23). These dates are called the **vernal equinox** and **autumnal equinox,** respectively. On these dates at the equator, the Sun reaches its highest **altitude** (angular distance above the horizon), which is directly overhead or 90° above the horizon, at noon.

At sunrise, when the Sun is rising above the horizon, the shadows of objects are long. In this investigation, there were no shadows for 90°, which represented the sun's noontime altitude at the equator on the equinox.

FOR FURTHER INVESTIGATION

The angular distance north or south of Earth's equator is called **latitude.** A project question might be, How does latitude affect sun shadows during the equinoxes?

Clues for Your Investigation

1. Determine the noontime altitude of the Sun at the equinox for different latitudes in the Northern and **Southern Hemispheres** (area south of the equator) by subtracting the latitude from 90°. Then repeat the original investigation, moving the flashlight in an arc from 0° to the calculated angles

above the horizon with your helper marking the shadow line. Label each line with the latitude. For example, at latitude 40°N, the flashlight would be held at an angle of 50° (90° – 40°) above the pencil on the southern side of the poster board. The shadow of the pencil would be on the northern side of the poster board. At 40°S, the noontime sun would be at an altitude 50° above the northern horizon.

2. Photographs of some or all of the flashlight positions at the different angles, as well as the labeled shadow lines, could be used to represent the results.

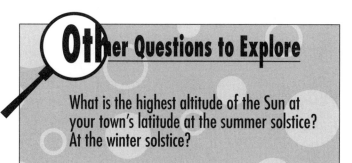

Other Questions to Explore

What is the highest altitude of the Sun at your town's latitude at the summer solstice? At the winter solstice?

REFERENCES AND PROJECT BOOKS

Asimov, Isaac. *Astronomy Projects.* Milwaukee: Gareth Stevens, 1996.

Mitton, Jacqueline, and Simon Mitton. *The Scholastic Encyclopedia of Space.* New York: Scholastic, 1998.

Mitton, Simon, and Jacqueline Mitton. *The Young Oxford Book of Astronomy.* New York: Oxford University Press, 1995.

Moché, Dinah L. *Astronomy: A Self-Teaching Guide.* New York: Wiley, 1996.

Steele, Philip. *Black Holes and Other Space Phenomena.* New York: Kingfisher Books, 1995.

VanCleave, Janice. *Janice VanCleave's A+ Projects in Astronomy.* New York: Wiley, 2001.

———. *Janice VanCleave's Astronomy for Every Kid.* New York: Wiley, 1991.

———. *Janice VanCleave's Solar System.* New York: Wiley, 2000.

Wood, Robert W. *Science for Kids: 39 Easy Astronomy Experiments.* Blue Ridge Summit, Pa.: Tab Books, 1991.

6 Escape

So You Want to Do a Project about **Satellites!**

LET'S EXPLORE

Purpose

To determine why satellites orbit Earth.

Materials

2 paper towels
9-inch (22.5-cm) plastic plate
BB
scissors
ruler
drinking straw
transparent tape

Procedure

1. Lay the paper towels on a table and set the plate in the middle of the towels. The towels are to keep the BB from rolling if dropped.
2. Cut and keep a 3-inch (7.5-cm) piece from the straw.
3. Lay the piece of straw across the plate as shown, with one end of the straw raised by the upper part of the rim of the plate and the other end resting on the plate near the lower part of the rim.
4. Tape the lower end of the piece of straw to the plate.
5. Insert the BB in the raised end of the straw and release it. Observe the movement of the BB.
6. Repeat step 5 three or more times.

Results

The BB exits the straw, hits the rim of the plate, and moves around the inside rim of the plate until it slows and stops.

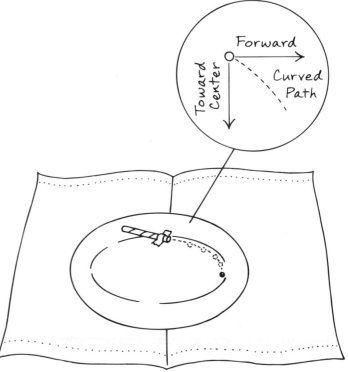

Why?

A **satellite** is a body that orbits (moves in a curved path around another object) a celestial body. This includes natural satellites, such as moons orbiting planets, as well as man-made satellites, such as weather satellites orbiting Earth. Satellites, like the BB in this investigation, are acted on by forward motion and a **centripetal force** (force on an object toward the center of its orbit). Man-made satellites are raised to a desired height above Earth and turned by rockets so that with additional rocket power they are launched so they orbit Earth. Thus, they have a forward motion **tangential** (touching at a single point) to the orbit. Earth's **gravity** is the force that pulls everything, including satellites, toward the center of Earth. Thus, gravity is the centripetal force acting on a satellite. Without gravity, the forward motion of a satellite would cause it to move in a straight path and fly out into space. Without forward motion, gravity would pull the satellites to Earth's surface.

In this investigation, the BB (satellite) left the straw with a forward motion and would have continued to move forward except for the force of the plate's rim. When the BB hit the rim, an inward force acts on the BB, moving it toward the center of the plate. The force of the rim represents gravity. The forward motion of the BB and the inward force of the rim resulted in the BB moving in a circular path. The action of forward motion and gravity are what make satellites orbit around Earth.

FOR FURTHER INVESTIGATION

In 1969, the spacecraft *Apollo 11* landed on the Moon. This craft at first orbited Earth. Why didn't gravity keep this craft in orbit around Earth? A project question might be, How can spacecraft escape Earth's gravity?

Clues for Your Investigation

1. Determine if the length and elevation of the straw can affect the forward motion of the BB. Repeat the original investigation using a full-length straw. The straw should be in the same position, with the upper end supported by the rim of the plate. Repeat the investigation again, raising the upper end.
2. Diagrams using arrows can be used to indicate the direction in which the satellite is launched and the direction of gravity. The wider the shaft and head of the arrow, the greater the speed and force of gravity.

Other Questions to Explore

1. What is a geosynchronous satellite?
2. How fast does a spacecraft have to travel to go into orbit around Earth?

REFERENCES AND PROJECT BOOKS

Englebert, Phillis, and Diane L. Dupuis. *The Handy Space Answer Book.* Detroit: Visible Ink Press, 1997.

Graham, Ian S. *All about Space.* Owings Mills, Md.: Southwater, 2000.

Moeschl, Richard. *Exploring the Sky.* Chicago: Chicago Review Press, 1993.

Paul, Richard. *A Handbook to the Universe.* Chicago: Chicago Review Press, 1993.

Steele, Philip. *Black Holes and Other Space Phenomena.* New York: Kingfisher Books, 1995.

VanCleave, Janice. *Janice VanCleave's A+ Projects in Astronomy.* New York: Wiley, 2001.

———. *Janice VanCleave's Astronomy for Every Kid.* New York: Wiley, 1991.

Wiese, Jim. *Cosmic Science.* New York: Wiley, 1997.

7 Morning Star

So You Want to Do a Project about **Venus!**

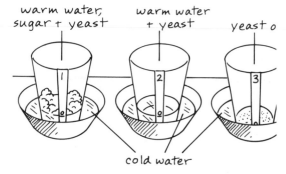

warm water, sugar + yeast

warm water + yeast

yeast o

cold water

LET'S EXPLORE

Purpose

To determine why Venus has phases.

Materials

lamp
pencil
4-inch (10-cm) Styrofoam ball
measuring tape
helper

Procedure

1. Set the lamp on a table and remove its shade. The lightbulb will be referred to as the lamp.
2. Insert about 1 inch (2.5 cm) of the pointed end of the pencil into the Styrofoam ball.
3. Darken the room except for the light from the lamp.
4. Holding the pencil, position the ball in front of but below the lamp.
5. At a slight angle, slowly move the ball counterclockwise halfway around the lamp, stopping when the ball is behind and above the lamp.
6. As you move the ball, make note of the changes in shape of the visible portion of the lighted side of the ball. Ask your helper to measure the width of the shadow cast on the ball when the ball is in front of, to the side of, and behind the lamp.

Results

In front of the lamp, the lighted side of the ball is not visible. As the ball moves from the front to the back of the lamp, the visible lighted part of the ball increases in size.

Why?

Galileo Galilei (1564–1642), an Italian astronomer, observed that the planet Venus undergoes **phases** (changes in the size and shape of the lighted side of a celestial body visible to observers on Earth). He used this information to show that Venus orbits the Sun and does not orbit Earth as many believed at that time. He observed that when Venus is almost fully sunlit, it appears to move behind the Sun as viewed from Earth and is out of sight. If it orbited Earth, when fully sunlit it would be on the opposite side of the sky from the Sun, as the Moon, which orbits Earth, is fully lit when it is on the opposite side of the sky from the Sun.

In this investigation, the ball represents Venus and the lamp (lightbulb) the Sun. Venus is an **inferior planet** (planet whose orbit is closer to the Sun than Earth's). There are two inferior planets, Mercury and Venus. During Venus's orbit around the Sun, as seen from Earth, Venus moves in front of and behind the Sun. When Venus is between Earth and the Sun, Venus is said to be in **inferior conjunction. Conjunction** occurs when two celestial bodies appear in the sky one under the other, but not one in front of the other. Venus's apparent separation from the Sun as viewed from Earth is so small that during inferior conjunction as well as **superior conjunction** (position of an inferior planet when it is on the opposite side of the Sun from Earth), the light of the Sun is so bright that Venus is not visible. While it appears that Venus passes directly in front of or directly behind the Sun, this occurs rarely and most of the time they just appear to be close.

During inferior conjunction, Venus is not visible because the side of the planet reflecting the Sun's light is facing away from Earth. Also, the bright light of the Sun in this position prevents the planet from being seen. Venus moves in a counterclockwise direction around the Sun. As Venus moves from inferior to superior conjunction, more of its lighted side faces Earth, thus Venus is said to be in a **waxing** (growing in size) phase. As the planet approaches a superior conjunction, it is almost fully sunlit, then it disappears because of the Sun's light.

During this movement from inferior to superior conjunction, Venus would appear to the west of the Sun in the sky. When Venus is far enough away from the Sun to rise above the horizon before the Sun in the morning, the planet is seen in the eastern sky. At this time, Venus appears to shine like a star and is called the "morning star."

FOR FURTHER INVESTIGATION

Sometimes Venus is seen above the western horizon in the evening and is called the "evening star." Do Venus's phases **wane** (decrease in size) when it moves from superior to inferior conjunction? A project question might be, What are the phases of Venus during one orbit?

Clues for Your Investigation

1. Repeat the investigation, moving the ball in a complete counterclockwise circle around the light.
2. Make note of the visible lighted side of the ball as it moves around the light. Diagram the different phases as Venus moves from inferior to superior conjunction, and then from superior to inferior conjunction.

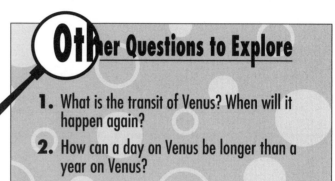

Other Questions to Explore

1. What is the transit of Venus? When will it happen again?
2. How can a day on Venus be longer than a year on Venus?

REFERENCES AND PROJECT BOOKS

Asimov, Isaac. *A Stargazer's Guide.* Milwaukee: Gareth Stevens, 1995.

Becklake, Sue. *Space.* New York: Dorling Kindersley, 1998.

Lafferty, Peter. *Science Facts: Space.* New York: Crescent Books, 1992.

Levy, David H. *Stars and Planets.* New York: Time-Life Books, 1998.

Mitton, Jacqueline. *Discovering the Planets.* New York: Troll, 1991.

Mitton, Simon, and Jacqueline Mitton. *The Young Oxford Book of Astronomy.* New York: Oxford University Press, 1995.

Moeschl, Richard. *Exploring the Sky.* Chicago: Chicago Review Press, 1993.

Nicolson, Cynthia Pratt. *The Planets.* Toronto: Kids Can Press, 1998.

VanCleave, Janice. *Janice VanCleave's A+ Projects in Astronomy.* New York: Wiley, 2001.

———. *Janice VanCleave's Astronomy for Every Kid.* New York: Wiley, 1991.

———. *Janice VanCleave's Solar System.* New York: Wiley, 2000.

Wood, Robert W. *Science for Kids: 39 Easy Astronomy Experiments.* Blue Ridge Summit, Pa.: Tab Books, 1991.

8 Splat!

So You Want to Do a Project about **Meteorites!**

LET'S EXPLORE

Purpose

To determine what happens when a meteorite hits Earth.

Materials

6 to 8 cups (1.5 to 2 L) sand (Cornmeal will work.)
large shoe box or comparable-size container
flat toothpick
2 fine-point felt-tip pens—1 black, 1 red
walnut-size piece of modeling clay
ruler

Procedure

1. Pour the sand into the box, and shake the box so that the surface of the sand is as level as possible.
2. Set the box of sand on the floor, then insert the toothpick vertically in the center of the sand. The tip of the toothpick should touch the bottom of the box.
3. Use the black pen to mark a line on the toothpick level with the surface of the sand. Remove the toothpick and set it aside.
4. Shape the clay into a ball.
5. Stand next to the box and hold the clay ball waist high above the center of the sand in the container. Drop the ball.
6. Carefully remove the ball from the sand so that you disturb the sand as little as possible.
7. Insert the toothpick in the center of the hole in the sand formed by the ball.
8. Use the red pen to mark a line on the toothpick level with the surface of the sand in the center of the hole. This mark

should be on the same side of the toothpick as the first mark.
9. Measure the distance between the two marks on the toothpick to determine the depth of the hole. Record the measurement in a Meteorite Hole Data table like the one shown.
10. Shake the box of sand to smooth its surface, and then repeat steps 5 to 9.
11. Repeat step 10 two or more times.

Results

The depth of the hole in the sand will vary depending on the size and weight of the clay ball. The author measured a hole ½ inch (1.25 cm) deep.

Why?

Meteroids are all the solid **debris** (remains of things that have been broken down) in our solar system orbiting the Sun. If a meteoroid enters Earth's **atmosphere** (blanket of gases surrounding a celestial body), it becomes so hot due to **friction** (a force that opposes the

METEORITE HOLE DATA

	Trial 1	Trial 2	Trial 3	Trial 4	Average
Depth, inches (cm)					

motion of an object whose surface is in contact with another object) with the atmosphere that it **vaporizes** (changes to a gas), or burns up, and light energy is produced. This streak of light is what you see when you see a shooting star. When a meteoroid enters the atmosphere, it is then referred to as a **meteor.** The streak of light is also called a meteor. If any part of the original meteoroid that entered the atmosphere reaches the surface of the Earth, it is then called a **meteorite.** Meteorites made of material similar to that found in the rocks on Earth's surface are called **stony meteorites.** This experiment demonstrates the results of gravity pulling a stony meteorite through Earth's atmosphere and into a surface of soft sand. On impact, the sand is pushed out of the way, creating an **impact crater** (bowl-shaped depression caused by the impact of a solid body).

Most meteorites range from a dust speck to slightly larger ones that strike Earth with no more energy than a falling hailstone. But about 50,000 years ago a meteorite about 150 feet (45 m) in diameter hit Earth with the energy of a nuclear weapon. The crater produced is ¾ mile (1.2 km) in diameter and 667 feet (200 m) deep. It is found in Arizona and is called the Barringer Meteorite Crater.

FOR FURTHER INVESTIGATION

Since meteoroids come from different celestial bodies, they are made of different materials. **Iron meteorites** contain about 90 percent iron and are almost three times as heavy as stony meteorites. Do heavier meteorites make bigger holes? A project question might be, How would the composition of a meteorite affect the size of its impact crater?

Clues for Your Investigation

1. Demonstrate the difference in the impact of a heavier meteorite by repeating the experiment using a heavier piece of clay. Make a second clay ball the same size as the first, but make it heavier by wrapping the clay around three to four metal washers. Be sure to drop the second clay ball from the same height as the first. Use a different color pen to mark the results on the toothpick. Compare the depth of the impact holes of the two types of meteorites.
2. Photograph the sand before and after impact. Display the photos to represent the results.

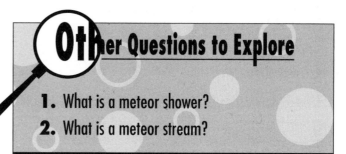

Other Questions to Explore

1. What is a meteor shower?
2. What is a meteor stream?

REFERENCES AND PROJECT BOOKS

Ardley, Neil. *The Science Book of Gravity.* New York: Harcourt Brace Jovanovich, 1992.

Asimov, Isaac. *Astronomy Projects.* Milwaukee: Gareth Stevens, 1996.

Becklake, Sue. *Space.* New York: Dorling Kindersley, 1998.

Redfern, Martin. *The Kingfisher Young People's Book of Space.* New York: Kingfisher Books, 1998.

Simon, Seymour. *Comets, Meteors, and Asteroids.* New York: Mulberry Books, 1994.

Snowden, Sheila. *The Young Astronomer.* London: Usborne, 1989.

VanCleave, Janice. *Janice VanCleave's A+ Projects in Earth Science.* New York: Wiley, 1998.

———. *Janice VanCleave's Astronomy for Every Kid.* New York: Wiley, 1991.

———. *Janice VanCleave's Solar System.* New York: Wiley, 2000.

Weise, Jim. *Cosmic Science.* New York: Wiley, 1997.

LET'S EXPLORE

Purpose

To determine the light-gathering power of a telescope.

Materials

drawing compass
ruler
unruled index card
sheet of black construction paper
¼-inch (0.63-cm) paper punch
glue

Procedure

1. Use the compass to draw a circle with a 2-inch (5-cm) diameter on the card.
2. Fold the black paper in half lengthwise twice.
3. Use the paper punch to cut through the four layers of paper. Save the four circles cut from the black paper.

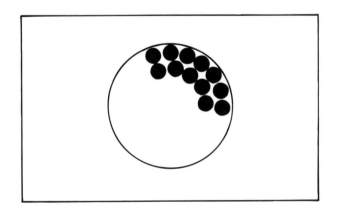

4. Glue the four black paper circles as close together as possible without overlapping their edges inside the circle drawn on the index card.

5. Repeat steps 3 and 4 until as much of the circle as possible is covered with a single layer of black paper circles. Count the number of circles used.

Results

The model contains about 64 circles. This is about how much more light a typical telescope can gather than your eye.

Why?

The **light-gathering power** of optical instruments such as telescopes is a measure of their **light amplification,** or how much brighter an object appears when viewed through an optical instrument than with your unaided dark-adapted eye. In the dark, the pupil **dilates** (enlarges) to a diameter of about ¼ inch (6.4 mm), about the size of one of the dark circles you punched out, and its light-gathering power increases. When the pupil is dilated, the eye has increased light-gathering power and the eye is said to be **dark adapted.**

In this investigation, the area of the 2-inch (50-mm) aperture of an optical instrument is compared to the area of the pupil of a dark-adapted eye. (An **aperture** is an opening in an optical instrument through which light enters.) The light-gathering power of a telescope's 2-inch (50-mm) aperture as compared to the aperture of your eye is about 64:1. This can be calculated from the diameters (*d*) of the apertures of the telescope and the pupil of your eye, using the following equation:

$$\frac{d^2 \text{ (telescope)}}{d^2 \text{ (eye)}} = \frac{2^2}{0.25^2} = \frac{4}{0.0625} = \frac{64}{1}$$

The number of circles needed to cover the 2-inch (50-mm) circle indicates the number of times more light-gathering power the instrument has as compared to the eye. The model shows that a telescope with a 2-inch (50-mm) diameter has about 64 times the light-gathering power of a dark-adapted eye. So, the light amplification of the telescope is about 64.

FOR FURTHER INVESTIGATION

Telescopes come in different sizes. Do distant objects appear brighter when viewed through a large telescope than when viewed through a small one? A project question might be, How can the light-gathering power of two telescopes be compared?

Clues for Your Investigation

1. Using a compass and an unruled 5-by-8-inch (12.5-by-20-cm) index card, draw a model of a telescope's 4-inch (100-mm) aperture. Fill the 4-inch (10-cm) -diameter circle with small black circles and count the total number of circles.
2. Use the equation in the original investigation to calculate the difference between the light-gathering powers of the 4-inch (100-mm) and 2-inch (50-mm) apertures.
3. Display the models as well as your calculations of light amplification for each.

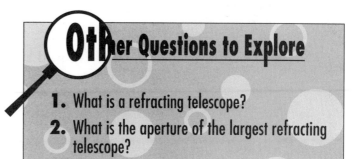

Other Questions to Explore

1. What is a refracting telescope?
2. What is the aperture of the largest refracting telescope?

REFERENCES AND PROJECT BOOKS

Asimov, Isaac. *A Stargazer's Guide.* Milwaukee: Gareth Stevens, 1995.

Graham, Ian S. *All about Space.* Owings Mills, Md.: Southwater, 2000.

Levy, David H. *The Sky.* New York: Cambridge University Press, 1995.

Matloff, Gregory L. *Telescope Power.* New York: Wiley, 1993.

Moché, Dinah L. *Astronomy: A Self-Teaching Guide.* New York: Wiley, 1996.

Ridpath, Ian. *Stars and Planets Atlas.* New York: Facts on File, 1997.

Snowden, Sheila. *The Young Astronomer.* London: Usborne, 1989.

VanCleave, Janice. *Janice VanCleave's A+ Projects in Astronomy.* New York: Wiley, 2001.

———. *Janice VanCleave's Astronomy for Every Kid.* New York: Wiley, 1991.

———. *Janice VanCleave's Constellations for Every Kid.* New York: Wiley, 1997.

10 Moon Phase

So You Want to Do a Project about the **Moon!**

Let's Explore

Purpose

To determine why the Moon appears completely dark during parts of the month.

Materials

paper clip
3-inch (7.5-cm) -diameter Styrofoam ball
12-inch (30-cm) piece of string
pencil
10-inch (25-cm) or larger cube-shaped box
serrated knife (requires adult help)
ruler
desk lamp
transparent tape
adult helper

Procedure

1. Push about three-fourths of the paper clip into the Styrofoam ball.
2. Tie one end of the string to the paper clip.
3. Use the pencil to make a small hole in the center of the top of the box. Put the ball inside the box and thread the free end of the string through the hole in the box.
4. Ask an adult to use the knife to cut a 2-inch (5-cm) square opening in the center of each of two opposite sides of the box. Label one opening "New."
5. Set the box on a table so that the hole is on the top. Put a desk lamp next to the box and position it so that the bulb is about 4 inches (10 cm) away from, and shining toward, the "New" opening in one side of the box.
6. In a darkened room, look through the other unlabeled viewing opening in the box. Pull the string to raise the Styrofoam ball until it blocks the light coming from the lamp, making the ball appear dark. Secure the string with tape.
7. Observe and make a diagram of the side of the ball that is facing you.

Results

The side of the Styrofoam ball facing you appears dark.

Why?

Like the Styrofoam ball, the Moon shines because it **reflects** (bounces back) light from the Sun. The side of the moon facing the Sun is always bright. The side away from the Sun is always dark. When the Moon in its orbit around Earth is in conjunction (one under the other) with the Sun, the side of the Moon facing Earth is dark. This dark, unlighted phase is referred to as the **new moon.** The new moon rises with the Sun in the east and sets with the Sun in the west.

For Further Investigation

As the Moon orbits Earth during the month, observers on Earth see different portions of the Moon reflecting light. The changes of the Moon's shape as seen from Earth are called phases of the Moon. A complete cycle of phases takes about 29½ days. A project question might be, What causes different amounts of the Moon to appear to be lighted during the month?

Clues for Your Investigation

1. The box from the original investigation can be used to model other phases of the Moon.
2. Repeat step 4 to cut an opening in each of the remaining two sides of the box. Label the opening to the right of the viewing opening "First Quarter" and label the remaining opening "Third Quarter."
3. Move the desk lamp so that it shines through the different openings. Be sure to look at the Styrofoam ball through the viewing opening each time.

MOON PHASE DATA

New Moon	First Quarter Moon	Third Quarter Moon

4. Make a drawing of the different phases seen when the lamp is shining through each of the openings in a Moon Phase Data table like the one shown.
5. Prepare a drawing of the positions of the Moon, Earth, and Sun during different moon phases as shown.

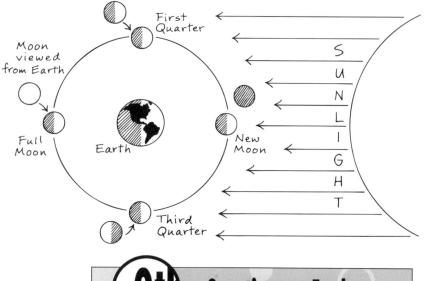

Other Questions to Explore

1. Why is the same side of the Moon always seen from Earth?
2. What is the Moon's albedo and why is it so large?
3. Why isn't there a solar eclipse at every new moon?

References and Project Books

Graham, Ian S. *The Best Book of the Moon.* New York: Kingfisher Books, 1999.

Koppeschaar, Carl. *Moon Handbook.* Chico, Calif.: Moon Publications, 1995.

Levy, David H. *The Sky.* New York: Cambridge University Press, 1995.

Matloff, Gregory L. *Telescope Power.* New York: Wiley, 1993.

Mitton, Simon, and Jacqueline Mitton. *The Young Oxford Book of Astronomy.* New York: Oxford University Press, 1995.

Snowden, Sheila. *The Young Astronomer.* London: Usborne, 1989.

VanCleave, Janice. *Janice VanCleave's A+ Projects in Astronomy.* New York: Wiley, 2001.

———. *Janice VanCleave's Astronomy for Every Kid.* New York: Wiley, 1991.

———. *Janice VanCleave's Solar System.* New York: Wiley, 2000.

Wiese, Jim. *Cosmic Science.* New York: Wiley, 1997.

Biology

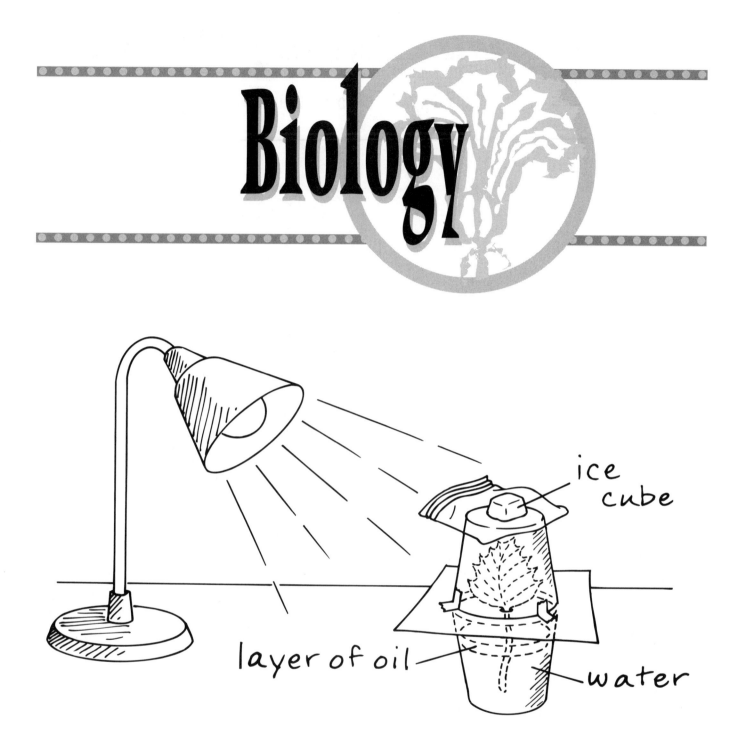

ice cube

layer of oil

water

Building Blocks

So You Want to Do a Project about **Cells!**

LET'S EXPLORE

Purpose

To discover the four basic parts of an animal cell.

Materials

package of lemon gelatin dessert mix
1-quart (1-L) resealable plastic bag
1-quart (1-L) bowl
large grape
5 peanuts (with or without their shells)
12-inch (30-cm) -square piece of white poster
   board
marker
adult helper

NOTE: This experiment requires a refrigerator.

Procedure

1. With adult assistance, make the lemon gelatin following the package directions. When the gelatin reaches room temperature, pour it into the bag. Seal the bag and put it in the refrigerator for 3 to 4 hours.
2. When the gelatin is firm, open the bag and, using your finger, insert the grape into the center of the gelatin. Insert the peanuts so that they are distributed evenly. This is your model cell.
3. Use the poster board and marker to make a stand-up legend for the model cell. Do this by folding the poster board in half. On one half of the poster board, draw the bag with its contents. Next to the bag, draw a cell, as shown, and label these parts: cell membrane, cytoplasm, nucleus, mitochondria.

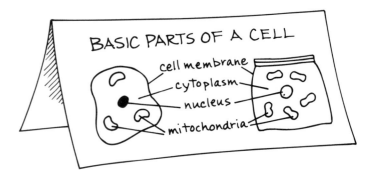

Place the legend card next to the model cell.

Results

You have made a model of four basic cell parts.

Why?

A **cell** is the smallest building block of most living things. All cells have a **cell membrane** (represented by the plastic bag), which is the thin outer skin that holds the cell together and allows materials to move into and out of the cell. **Organelles** are structures within cells that have specific functions, such as the nucleus and mitochondria. The **nucleus** (grape) is a spherical or oval-shaped body, often in the center of the cell, that controls all cell activity. The peanuts floating in the gelatin represent the **mitochondria** (singular **mitochondrion**), which are the power stations of the cell. In the mitochondria, food and oxygen combine to produce the energy needed for the cell to work and live. The **cytoplasm** (gelatin) is technically the entire region between the nucleus and the cell membrane. It is commonly identified as the clear, jellylike material in which the cell parts float.

The four common parts of an animal cell—cell membrane, cytoplasm, mitochondria, and nucleus—all work together and are necessary for the life of the cell.

For Further Investigation

Animals and plants are very different in their physical appearances. Do you think their cells are different as well? A project question might be, How do plant and animal cells compare?

Clues for Your Investigation

Make a model plant cell similar to the model animal cell you made in the original investigation. Use different things to represent the different parts of a plant cell. Model animal and plant cells can be displayed along with a labeled diagram or a legend for the cell parts in each.

Other Questions to Explore

1. What other organelles are present in animal cells in addition to those shown in the simplified model cell?

2. How do the cells in different parts of a plant, such as those for leaves, stems, and roots, differ?

3. How do different animal cells, such as those for nerves, fat, muscle, and blood, differ?

References and Project Books

Barnes, Kate, and Steve Weston. *The Human Body*. New York: Barnes & Noble, 1997.

Chisholm, Jane. *Introduction to Biology*. London: Usborne, 1984.

Parker, Steve. *How the Body Works*. Pleasantville, N.Y.: Reader's Digest, 1994.

VanCleave, Janice. *Janice VanCleave's Animals*. New York: Wiley, 1992.

———. *Janice VanCleave's Biology for Every Kid*. New York: Wiley, 1990.

———. *Janice VanCleave's The Human Body for Every Kid*. New York: Wiley, 1995.

———. *Janice VanCleave's Plants*. New York: Wiley, 1996.

Walker, Richard. *The Children's Atlas of the Human Body*. Brookfield, Conn.: Millbrook Press, 1994.

Weiner, Esther. *The Incredible Human Body*. New York: Scholastic, 1996.

Wood, Robert W. *Science for Kids: 39 Easy Plant Biology Experiments*. Blue Ridge Summit, Pa.: Tab Books, 1991.

LET'S EXPLORE

Purpose

To collect leaf rubbings.

Materials

2 or 3 leaves from different plants
3 or 4 sheets of newspaper
2 sheets of white copy paper
crayon

Procedure

1. With adult permission, collect the leaves from different trees and/or bushes. *CAUTION: Do not pick leaves from plants such as poison ivy or poison oak. Ask for adult assistance if you are not sure that a leaf is safe to handle.*
2. Place the sheets of newspaper on a table to protect the table's surface.
3. Arrange the leaves on one sheet of copy paper so that their rough sides are up and the leaves do not overlap.
4. Cover the leaves with the second sheet of copy paper.

leaves between sheets of copy paper

5. With firm pressure, rub the crayon across the paper over the leaves.

Results

A colored rubbing of each leaf is made.

Why?

More of the crayon is rubbed off by the rough edges and ridges, so these features of the leaves show up as darker areas on the paper. The **petiole** (stalk) of a leaf contains long, tubelike structures that are called **veins** when they branch out in different directions when they reach the **blade** (large part of a leaf). If the leaf of a plant consists of a single blade, it is called a **simple leaf,** although the edges may be indented in many ways. If the leaf blade is divided into two or more separate parts, the leaf is a **compound leaf.** Each leaflike part of a compound leaf is called a **leaflet.**

The pattern of large veins in the blade is called the **venation** of the leaf. There are two basic types of venation: parallel and netted. In leaves with **parallel venation,** such as those of a lily or grass, the large veins are parallel to each other and the edge of the leaf. In leaves with **netted venation,** such as those of a sunflower or oak, the veins branch and rebranch in the blade.

Netted venation can be grouped into two types: palmate and pinnate. If the large veins in netted venation all start at the end of the petiole and extend through the blade like fingers from the palm of a hand, the netted venation is called **palmate venation.** The leaves of the sycamore and sugar maple trees have palmate venation. If a single large vein runs through the center of the leaf and smaller veins branch from it in a feather shape, this type of netted venation is called **pinnate venation.** The leaves of oak, elm, and apple trees have pinnate venation.

Compound leaves, like veins, can have a palmate or pinnate pattern. If the leaflets fan out from a common point at the petiole, such as those of a clover, horse chestnut, or poison ivy, they are called **palmately compound.** If the leaflets are attached along a central stalk, such as those of a rose, ash, walnut, or hickory, they are called **pinnately compound.**

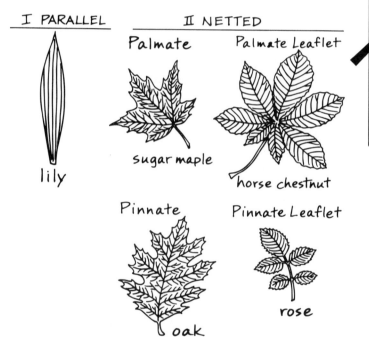

I PARALLEL — II NETTED

Palmate — sugar maple
Palmate Leaflet — horse chestnut
Pinnate — oak
Pinnate Leaflet — rose
lily

FOR FURTHER INVESTIGATION

Did the leaves you found all have the same basic pattern, or were they different? How many different kinds of leaf patterns can you find? A project question might be, How many different leaf patterns can be found in my neighborhood?

Clues for Your Investigation

Collect more leaves from your neighborhood and make rubbings of them. Compare the vein patterns on the leaves. Group them by vein pattern type. You may want to use a plant field guide to identify the plant that each leaf comes from. Display the leaf rubbings arranged and labeled by type.

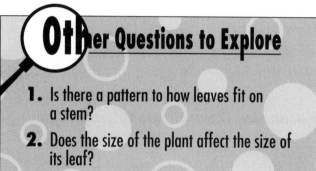

Other Questions to Explore

1. Is there a pattern to how leaves fit on a stem?
2. Does the size of the plant affect the size of its leaf?

REFERENCES AND PROJECT BOOKS

Althea. *Trees and Leaves.* New York: Troll, 1990.

Burnie, David. *How Nature Works.* Pleasantville, N.Y.: Reader's Digest, 1991.

Burton, Jane, and Kim Taylor. *The Nature and Science of Leaves.* Milwaukee: Gareth Stevens, 1997.

Forey, Pam. *Wild Flowers of North America.* San Diego: Thunder Bay Press, 1994.

Hershey, David R. *Plant Biology Science Projects.* New York: Wiley, 1995.

Kowalski, Kathiann M. *The Everything Kids' Nature Book.* Holbrook, Mass.: Adams Media Corporation, 2000.

Suzuki, David. *Looking at Plants.* New York: Wiley, 1991.

VanCleave, Janice. *Janice VanCleave's Biology for Every Kid.* New York: Wiley, 1990.

————. *Janice VanCleave's Plants.* New York: Wiley, 1996.

————. *Janice VanCleave's Science around the Year.* New York: Wiley, 2000.

LET'S EXPLORE

Purpose

To demonstrate transpiration, the loss of water from leaves.

Materials

two 10-ounce (300-mL) plastic cups
tap water
pen
5-inch (12.5-cm) -square piece of poster board
sprig with 1 leaf and at least a 4-inch (10-cm) stem
scissors
1 teaspoon (5 mL) cooking oil
transparent tape
desk lamp
ruler
ice cube
resealable plastic bag
adult helper

Procedure

1. Fill one of the cups about three-fourths full with water.
2. Ask an adult to use the pen to make a hole in the center of the poster board.
3. Push the stem of the sprig through the hole until the bottom of the leaf rests on the poster board.
4. Place the poster board, leaf side up, on the cup of water. The stem should be near but not touching the bottom of the cup. Trim the stem with scissors if it is too long.
5. Tilt one side of the poster board just enough to allow you to pour the oil into the cup, but do not let the stem come out of the water. You do not want the oil to get on the cut end of the stem because it can close off the openings in the stem.

6. Lower the poster board. Put the remaining cup upside down over the poster board to cover the leaf. The entire rim of this cup should rest on the poster board. Secure the rim to the poster board with tape.
7. Move the cups so that the top cup is about 12 inches (30 cm) from the bulb of the desk lamp.
8. Put the ice cube in the resealable plastic bag and place it on top of the top cup.
9. Lift the plastic bag every half hour for 3 or more hours and observe any water collected on the inside surface of the top cup. Observe the lamp side, the side opposite the lamp, and the top. Record your observations in a Transpiration Data table like the one shown.

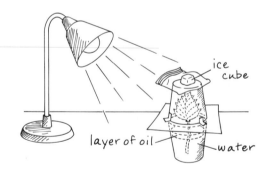

Results

Tiny droplets of water appear on the inside of the cup. More droplets appear on the top near the ice cube than on other parts of the glass.

Why?

Plants **absorb** (soak up) water from the soil through their roots. This water moves up the stem to the leaves, where about 90 percent is lost by **evaporation** (the process by which a liquid changes to a gas). The **water vapor**

TRANSPIRATION DATA

Cup's Surface	Time (hours)						
	Start	½	1	1½	2	2½	3
Lamp Side							
Opposite Lamp							
Top							

(water in gas form) leaves the leaf through **stomata,** which are tiny openings in leaves through which gases can exit or enter. A single corn plant may lose more than 2 quarts (2 L) of water per day, and 1 acre (2.47 ha) of corn can lose more than 1 million quarts (liters) during a growing season. This process by which plants lose water from their leaves by evaporation is called **transpiration.**

In this investigation, the water vapor lost by the leaves through transpiration is collected in the plastic cup. The ice as well as the air in the room cools the surface of the cup. When the water vapor touches the cool surface of the cup, **condensation** (the process by which a gas changes to a liquid) occurs and water droplets form on the inside of the cup. The side of the cup next to the ice is cooler than the side facing the lamp, so more water droplets form on the cooler side.

FOR FURTHER INVESTIGATION

Do plants lose more water during the daytime or nighttime? A project question might be, How does light affect the volume of water lost by transpiration?

Clues for Your Investigation

1. Repeat the experiment, preparing 2 two-cup setups with stems. Set the cups at an equal distance from the light. (Putting the cups at an equal distance from the light helps control the temperature so that it is not a factor.) Use boxes to cover one of the two-cup-with-stem setups.

2. Compare the amount of liquid collected on the inside of each cup over the same period of time.

3. For the most accurate results, do four or more tests with and without light.

Other Questions to Explore

1. Do different plants vary in their rate of transpiration?

2. What is turgor pressure and how does it affect transpiration?

3. Would sunlight at different times of the day affect the rate at which a leaf transpires?

REFERENCES AND PROJECT BOOKS

Bonnet, Robert L., and G. Daniel Keen. *Botany: 49 Science Fair Projects.* Blue Ridge Summit, Pa.: Tab Books, 1989.

——. *Botany: 49 More Science Fair Projects.* Blue Ridge Summit, Pa.: Tab Books, 1991.

Chisholm, Jane. *Introduction to Biology.* London: Usborne, 1984.

Franklin, Sharon. *The Inside Story.* Glenview, Ill.: Good Year Books, 1995.

Suzuki, David. *Looking at Plants.* New York: Wiley, 1991.

VanCleave, Janice. *Janice VanCleave's Biology for Every Kid.* New York: Wiley, 1990.

——. *Janice VanCleave's Plants.* New York: Wiley, 1996.

Wood, Robert W. *Science for Kids: 39 Easy Plant Biology Experiments.* Blue Ridge Summit, Pa.: Tab Books, 1991.

14 In and Out

So You Want to Do a Project about **Osmosis!**

LET'S EXPLORE

PURPOSE

To demonstrate osmosis.

Materials

2 small bowls
tap water
vegetable knife (requires adult help)
potato
adult helper

Procedure

1. Fill one of the bowls half full with water.
2. Ask your adult helper to cut four slices about ¼ inch (0.63 cm) thick from the potato.
3. Test the firmness of each potato slice by holding it in your hands and trying to bend it. Do not break the slices.
4. Place two potato slices in each bowl.
5. After 30 minutes, pick up the potato slices one at a time from the water with your fingers. Again test their firmness by trying to bend them.
6. Repeat step 5, using the potato slices that were not placed in water.
7. How does the firmness of the potato slices soaked in water compare to the firmness of those not soaked in water?

Results

The slices not soaked in water do not change or decrease only slightly in firmness. The potato slices soaked in water are firmer and do not bend easily.

Why?

Osmosis is the movement of water through a type of **membrane** (thin layer of animal or plant tissue) called a **semipermeable membrane.** This membrane selectively allows materials, such as water, to pass through. Each cell in the potato has a semipermeable membrane around it.

Inside each potato cell is a **solution,** which is a mixture of a **solute** (the substance that is dissolved) and a **solvent** (the substance that does the dissolving). When a solute **dissolves,** it is broken into small particles and mixes thoroughly with a solvent. The cell solution is made of water (the solvent) with different solutes dissolved in it. Tap water is a solution with a very low **concentration** (the amount of solute in a solution) of solutes. In this investigation, the solution outside the cell (tap water) has a lower concentration of solute and a higher concentration of water than the solution inside the cell, therefore the tap water is called a **hypotonic solution.** When a cell is placed in a hypotonic solution, water moves into the cell. This increases the pressure inside the cell. Water moves through a semipermeable membrane from the side with a low solute concentration to the side with a high solute concentration.

The pressure inside a plant cell due to the presence of water is called **turgor pressure.** As the water inside the cells increases, the turgor pressure increases, and the water-soaked potato slices feel firm. The turgor pressure of the potato slices not placed in water may have decreased slightly due to a loss of water as the water from inside the potato cells moved out of the cells.

FOR FURTHER INVESTIGATION

If the solution outside the potato cells has a higher concentration of solute and a lower water concentration than the solution inside the cells, the outer solution is called a **hypertonic solution.** A project question might be, How does soaking potato cells in a hypertonic solution affect turgor pressure?

Clues for Your Investigation

1. Repeat the investigation, adding salt to the water in the bowl. Since you do not know the concentration of the solute inside the potato, you can have several bowls of water and use varying amounts of salt in each.
2. Design a way to measure the results, such as how far the slice will bend before breaking.

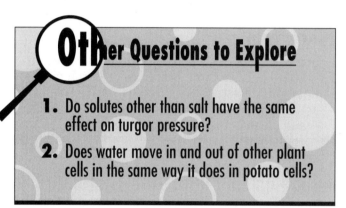

Other Questions to Explore

1. Do solutes other than salt have the same effect on turgor pressure?
2. Does water move in and out of other plant cells in the same way it does in potato cells?

REFERENCES AND PROJECT BOOKS

Bonnet, Robert L., and G. Daniel Keen. *Botany: 49 More Science Fair Projects.* Blue Ridge Summit, Pa.: Tab Books, 1991.

Chisholm, Jane. *Introduction to Biology.* London: Usborne, 1984.

Hershey, David R. *Plant Biology Science Projects.* New York: Wiley, 1995.

VanCleave, Janice. *Janice VanCleave's Biology for Every Kid.* New York: Wiley, 1990.

———. *Janice VanCleave's Plants.* New York: Wiley, 1996.

15 Snares

So You Want to Do a Project about **Spiders!**

LET'S EXPLORE

PURPOSE

To collect and examine a spiderweb.

Materials

orb web (wheel-shaped web with spokes, often found between tree branches or porch pillars)
field guide to spiders
small round plastic container, such as an empty and clean cottage cheese or margarine container
scissors
one-hole paper punch
index card
ruler
adult helper

Procedure

CAUTION: Make sure the spider isn't in the web before doing the investigation.

1. Have an adult help you find an orb web. Use a spider field guide to assist you in identifying the orb web, which looks like spokes of thread extending from the center and connected by spirals of thread. These webs can be found stretched between two structures, such as two trees.
2. Place the mouth of the container against the spiderweb.
3. Push the container forward to break off the part of the web covering the mouth of the container. Use the scissors to cut web strands so that the web is stretched across the mouth of the container.
4. Set the container on a table.
5. Using the paper punch, cut out 10 or more circles from the index card.

6. Holding your hand about 4 inches (10 cm) above the threads of the web, drop the paper circles one at a time, spacing them apart if possible.
7. Turn the cup upside down and gently shake it.

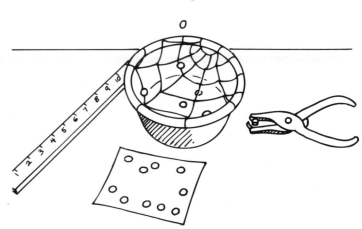

Results

Some of the paper circles stick to the threads and do not come loose even when the container is shaken.

Why?

The threads in a spiderweb are made of silk produced inside the spider's body. The silk flows out of tiny holes in the **spinnerets** (silk-spinning organs that are short fingerlike structures located near the end of the underside of a spider's abdomen). Some spider silk dries when the air touches it, and some silk stays wet and sticky. The sticky threads are made from a combination of dry and sticky silk. First a dry thread is made and put into place. Then the spinnerets move in fingerlike motion as they coat the dry silk thread with sticky silk. The spider then uses the claws on its legs to pluck the thread. The plucking causes the liquid silk to separate into tiny beads along the thread. The paper circles in this investigation, like insects, can get stuck to these sticky threads and can be unable to get loose. Captured insects are eaten by the spider.

FOR FURTHER INVESTIGATION

Spiders do not get stuck in their own webs. A project question might be, Why doesn't a spider get stuck in its web?

Clues for Your Investigation

1. How can different types of threads help keep the spider from sticking? Use the eraser of a pencil to test the stickiness of the different threads of the web-covered container from the original investigation. Use a magnifying lens to observe the appearance of the threads. A diagram showing any difference in the threads can be displayed.

2. Do spiders have something on their feet that keeps them from sticking to their web? Find out more about spiders' feet. Design a demonstration of how their special feet can help them move around on their sticky webs.

Other Questions to Explore

1. How strong are spiderwebs?
2. How does dust affect the stickiness of a spiderweb?
3. What are the different kinds of spiderwebs?

REFERENCES AND PROJECT BOOKS

Cain, Nancy Woodard. *Animal Behavior Science Projects.* New York: Wiley, 1995.

Kneidel, Sally. *Pet Bugs.* New York: Wiley, 1994.

———. *More Pet Bugs.* New York: Wiley, 1999.

Levi, Herbert W. *Spiders and Their Kin.* New York: Golden Press, 1990.

Milner, Lorus J. *National Audubon Society Field Guide to North American Insects and Spiders.* New York: Knopf, 1980.

Parsons, Alexandra. *Amazing Spiders.* New York: Knopf, 1990.

Robertson, Matthew. *Insects and Spiders.* Pleasantville, N.Y.: Reader's Digest, 2000.

VanCleave, Janice. *Janice VanCleave's Biology for Every Kid.* New York: Wiley, 1990.

———. Janice VanCleave's *Insects and Spiders.* New York: Wiley, 1998.

16 Identify

So You Want to Do a Project about **Fingerprints!**

LET'S EXPLORE

Purpose

To collect and identify fingerprint types.

Materials

pencil
2 white unruled index cards
transparent tape
magnifying lens

Procedure

1. Rub the lead of the pencil back and forth across one of the index cards. Then, rub your index finger across the pencil mark.
2. Cover your smudged fingertip with a piece of transparent tape. Press the tape firmly against your fingertip.
3. Carefully remove the tape and press the sticky side against the other index card.
4. Examine the pattern on the tape by looking at it through the magnifying lens.
5. Identify the pattern formed by your fingerprint by comparing it with the three basic fingerprint patterns: whorl, loop, and arch.

BASIC FINGERPRINT PATTERNS

whorl   loop   arch

Results

A copy of your fingerprint is left on the sticky side of the tape.

Why?

Your body has two layers of skin. The outer layer of skin is called the **epidermis,** and the inner layer is called the **dermis.** The boundary between the dermis and the epidermis is not straight and smooth but consists of small folds. These folds produce a series of ridges and grooves in areas where the skin is thick—the palm of the hand, the sole of the foot, and the fingertip, for example. The patterns formed by the ridges of the fingertips are called **fingerprints.** There are three basic fingerprint patterns—whorl, loop, and arch—but no two people have been found with exactly the same fingerprints, not even identical twins.

FOR FURTHER INVESTIGATION

Since your hands are mirror images of each other, do you think the fingerprints of your left hand mirror the fingerprints of your right hand? A project question might be, How do fingerprints of two hands of a person compare?

Clues for Your Investigation

1. Repeat the original investigation, examining the prints of each fingertip.
2. Collect fingerprints from as many different people as possible and make comparisons of the prints of their two hands.
3. Fingerprints of each hand can be collected and displayed.

Other Questions to Explore

1. Family members generally look alike; are their fingerprints similar?
2. How do the fingerprints of identical twins differ?

REFERENCES AND PROJECT BOOKS

Allison, Linda. *Blood and Guts.* New York: Little, Brown, 1976.

Beckelman, Laurie. *The Human Body.* Pleasantville, N.Y.: Reader's Digest, 1999.

Parker, Steve. *How the Body Works.* Pleasantville, N.Y.: Reader's Digest, 1994.

———. *The Human Body.* Brookfield, Conn.: Copper Beech Books, 1995.

Silver, Donald M., and Patricia J. Wynne. *The Body Book.* New York: Scholastic, 1993.

Stein, Sara. *The Body Book.* New York: Workman, 1992.

Suzuki, David. *Looking at the Body.* New York: Wiley, 1991.

VanCleave, Janice. *Janice VanCleave's Biology for Every Kid.* New York: Wiley, 1990.

———. *Janice VanCleave's The Human Body for Every Kid.* New York: Wiley, 1995.

Walker, Richard. *The Children's Atlas of the Human Body.* Brookfield, Conn.: Millbrook Press, 1994.

Walpole, Brenda. *Pocket Book of the Human Body.* New York: Wanderer Books, 1987.

Wellnitz, William R. *Homemade Slime and Rubber Bones!* Blue Ridge Summit, Pa.: Tab Books, 1993.

17 Foamy

So You Want to Do a Project about **Microbes!**

Let's Explore

Purpose

To determine the effect that yeast has on sugar.

Materials

3 small cereal bowls
cold and warm tap water
masking tape
three 10-ounce (300-mL) plastic cups
marker
2 teaspoons (10 mL) sugar
1-teaspoon (5-mL) measuring spoon
3 teaspoons (15 mL) dry yeast
¼-cup (63-mL) measuring cup
2 spoons
timer
ruler

Procedure

1. Fill the bowls half full with cold water.
2. Place a piece of masking tape up the side of each cup from bottom to top. At the top of the strips of masking tape, number the cups from 1 to 3.
3. In cup 1, combine the sugar and 1 teaspoon (5 mL) of yeast.
4. Put 1 teaspoon (5 mL) of yeast in each of the other cups.

5. Add ¼ cup (63 mL) of warm water to cups 1 and 2 only. Stir, using a different spoon for each cup.
6. On the masking tape, mark the level of the contents of each cup and label the marks 0.

7. Set one cup in each bowl of water.
8. Mark the level of the contents of the cup on the tape every 5 minutes for 30 minutes.
9. Measure the level of each mark on the tape and record it in a Foamy Data table like the one shown.

FOAMY DATA

	Level of Cup Contents, inches (cm)						
Cup Number	After 0 Minutes	After 5 Minutes	After 10 Minutes	After 15 Minutes	After 20 Minutes	After 25 Minutes	After 30 Minutes
1							
2							
3							

Results

Foam forms on the surface of the liquid in cup 1 and increases in level over time. The final level and the length of time to achieve that level can vary. No foam appears on the surface of the liquid in cup 2 or on the dry yeast in cup 3.

Why?

Microbes such as yeast are tiny living things visible only with a microscope, such as yeast. **Yeasts** are single-celled **fungi,** which are plantlike **organisms** (living things) that cannot produce their own food. Dry yeast is a type of yeast that has been **dehydrated** (has had the water removed). In this investigation, the dry yeast is **hydrated** (has had water added), which restores its ability to function normally. The sugar in the water in cup 1 provides a needed food source. The yeast in this cup **digests** (breaks food into smaller parts) the sugar, producing alcohol, carbon dioxide gas, and energy needed for life and reproduction. The process by which yeast digests sugar is called **fermentation.** The yeast in water alone in cup 2 does not have food, so it has nothing to digest and will not live. The yeast in cup 3 remains dry and inactive.

FOR FURTHER INVESTIGATION

The dough for yeast bread is put in a warm place to rise. Would the dough rise in a cool place? A project question might be, How does temperature affect fermentation by yeast?

Clues for Your Investigation

1. Repeat the original investigation, preparing three sets of cups. Place the sets in bowls of water with different temperatures: icy tap water, cold tap water, and hot tap water. To make sure the water remains icy and hot, add ice and change the hot water as needed. *CAUTION: Ask an adult to fill the bowls with hot water and to supervise handling of the bowls of hot water.*

2. For best results, repeat the investigation four or more times.

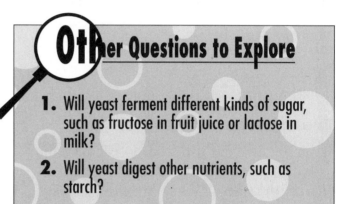

Other Questions to Explore

1. Will yeast ferment different kinds of sugar, such as fructose in fruit juice or lactose in milk?

2. Will yeast digest other nutrients, such as starch?

REFERENCES AND PROJECT BOOKS

Ardley, Neil. *The Science Book of Things That Grow.* New York: Harcourt, Brace, 1991.

D'Amico, Joan, and Karen Eich Drummond. *The Science Chef.* New York: Wiley, 1995.

Gibson, Gary. *Science for Fun Experiments.* Brookfield, Conn.: Copper Beech Books, 1996.

Levine, Shar, and Leslie Johnstone. *Silly Science.* New York: Wiley, 1995.

Stein, Sara. *The Science Book.* New York: Workman, 1980.

VanCleave, Janice. *Janice VanCleave's Biology for Every Kid.* New York: Wiley, 1990.

———. *Janice VanCleave's Food and Nutrition for Every Kid.* New York: Wiley, 1999.

 **Oops!**

So You Want to Do a Project about **Reaction Time!**

LET'S EXPLORE

Purpose

To determine how to measure reaction time.

Materials

table and chair
ruler
helper

Procedure

1. Sit on the chair with your forearm on the tabletop and your writing hand extended over the edge of the tabletop.
2. Ask your helper to hold the ruler so that the bottom of the stick (the zero end) is just above your hand.
3. Place your thumb and index finger on either side of, but not touching, the bottom of the ruler.
4. Ask your helper to drop the ruler through your fingers without telling you when it is going to be dropped.
5. After the ruler is released, try to catch it as quickly as possible between your thumb and fingers.
6. Observe the number on the ruler just above your thumb. Record this number as the reaction distance.

Results

The distance the ruler falls varies with each individual.

Why?

Reaction time is the time it takes you to respond to a **stimulus,** which is something that causes an organism to react. In this experiment, your reaction time was how long it took you to catch the falling ruler (stimulus). The greater the reaction time, the greater the reaction distance. In this project, the reaction distance is used to indicate the reaction time.

Reaction distance will vary with individuals because when the ruler begins to fall, a message is sent to the brain. Like a computer, the brain takes this input information and, in fractions of a second, sends a message telling the muscles in the hand to **contract** (shorten or be made smaller by drawing together). The distance the ruler falls varies for each individ-

ual depending on the time it takes for these messages to be sorted out by the brain and the output message to be received by the hand's muscles. **Nerves,** which are bundles of cells, send messages throughout the body. The nerves in the eye start this relay of messages. The first stop is in the largest section of the brain, called the **cerebrum.** The cerebrum is where all thoughts occur and where input from **sensory** (having to do with sight, smell, hearing, taste, and/or touch) nerves is interpreted. The cerebrum sends a message (nerve impulse) to another section of the brain, called the **cerebellum.** The cerebellum brings together all the muscle actions that are necessary to grasp the ruler. Reaction time does not have anything to do with how smart you are; instead, it compares differences in hand-eye coordination.

FOR FURTHER INVESTIGATION

Learning can occur when actions are repeated. Can a person learn to catch the ruler faster and improve the reaction time? A project question might be, How does practice affect reaction time?

Clues for Your Investigation

1. Repeat the investigation 10 or more times and have others perform the experiment as many times.
2. Record the results in a Reaction Time Data table like the one shown.

3. Create a line graph with each person's results plotted in a different color ink.
4. Display the table and graph as part of your project.

Other Questions to Explore

1. Does your writing hand have the same reaction time as your other hand?
2. Does reaction time vary with age?
3. Does reaction time vary with gender?

REFERENCES AND PROJECT BOOKS

Allison, Linda. *Blood and Guts.* New York: Little, Brown, 1976.

Beckelman, Laurie. *The Human Body.* Pleasantville, N.Y.: Reader's Digest, 1999.

Parker, Steve. *The Brain and Nervous System.* New York: Franklin Watts, 1990.

————. *How the Body Works.* Pleasantville, N.Y.: Reader's Digest, 1994.

————. *The Human Body.* Brookfield, Conn.: Copper Beech Books, 1995.

Schultz, Ron. *Looking inside the Brain.* Santa Fe, N.M.: John Muir Publications, 1992.

VanCleave, Janice. *Janice VanCleave's Animals.* New York: Wiley, 1992.

————. *Janice VanCleave's The Human Body for Every Kid.* New York: Wiley, 1995.

Wiese, Jim. *Head to Toe Science.* New York: Wiley, 2000.

REACTION TIME DATA

Names	Distance, inches (cm)									
	Trial 1	Trial 2	Trial 3	Trial 4	Trial 5	Trial 6	Trial 7	Trial 8	Trial 9	Trial 10
Laura										
Kate										
John										

19 Tasty

So You Want to Do a Project about **Taste!**

Let's Explore

Purpose

To discover what part of the tongue best detects sweet tastes.

Materials

1 teaspoon (5 mL) table sugar
paper plate
4 clean cotton swabs
glass of tap water
mirror

Procedure

CAUTION: Never taste substances during an experiment unless you are sure that these substances do not contain harmful chemicals or materials.

1. Pour the sugar into the paper plate.
2. Moisten one end of each cotton swab with water by dipping them in the glass of water. Then lay these ends on the sugar in the plate.
3. Look in the mirror and locate on your tongue the four areas—A, B, C, and D—shown in the figure.
4. Hold one of the cotton swabs and touch the wet end to area A on your tongue. Note any sweetness you taste. As a method of comparing sweetness, use a scale of 1, 2, 3, 4, and 5, with 1 being the least sweet.
5. Drink a small amount of water from the glass to rinse the sugar out of your mouth.
6. Record your results as trial 1 in a Sugar Tasting Data table like the one shown.
7. Repeat steps 4 through 6, recording the results as trials 2, 3, and 4. Average the trials and record in the Sugar Tasting Data table.

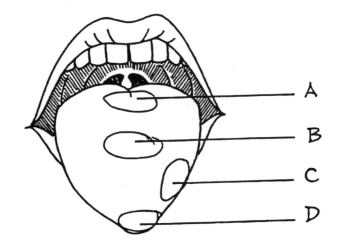

8. Repeat steps 4 through 7 with the remaining cotton swabs, touching the remaining areas on your tongue.

SUGAR TASTING DATA

Testing Area	Trial 1	Trial 2	Trial 3	Trial 4	Average
A					
B					
C					
D					

Results

Sweet tastes are best tasted on the tip of the tongue, in area D.

Why?

Taste buds are groups of sensory cells on the tongue and the roof and back of your mouth that are responsible for the sense of taste. Most of your taste buds are located on the tip, sides, and back of your tongue. Taste buds detect four main tastes—sweet, salt, sour, and bitter. While each taste bud can detect more than one taste, each is best at detecting one of the primary tastes. The taste buds that are best at detecting sweet tastes are located on the tip of the tongue.

FOR FURTHER INVESTIGATION

Artificial sweeteners are said to be sweeter than natural sugar. A project question might be, How do artificial sweeteners and natural sugar compare in sweetness?

Clues for Your Investigation

1. Use a marker to divide a plate into three sections. Label the sections "NutraSweet," "Sweet'n Low," and "Sugar."
2. Open the packets of artificial sweeteners and sugar and pour them in the labeled areas of the plate.
3. Repeat the investigation, placing the cotton swabs on only the tip of your tongue.
4. Record the results in a Tasting Data table like the one shown.

TASTING DATA

Sweetener	Trial 1	Trial 2	Trial 3	Trial 4	Average
Sugar					
NutraSweet					
Sweet'n Low					

Other Questions to Explore

1. Where on your tongue are these tastes best detected: salt, bitter, and sour?
2. How does smell affect the taste of foods?

REFERENCES AND PROJECT BOOKS

Barnes, Kate, and Steve Weston. *The Human Body.* New York: Barnes & Noble, 1997.

Beckelman, Laurie. *The Human Body.* Pleasantville, N.Y.: Reader's Digest, 1999.

Cobb, Vicki. *How to Really Fool Yourself.* New York: Wiley, 1999.

Ontario Science Centre. *Scienceworks: 65 Experiments That Introduce the Fun and Wonder of Science.* Reading, Mass.: Addison-Wesley, 1987.

Parker, Steve. *How the Body Works.* Pleasantville, N.Y.: Reader's Digest, 1994.

———. *The Human Body.* Brookfield, Conn.: Copper Beech Books, 1995.

———. *Touch, Taste, and Smell.* New York: Franklin Watts, 1982.

Stein, Sara. *The Body Book.* New York: Workman, 1992.

Suzuki, David. *Looking at Senses.* New York: Wiley, 1991.

VanCleave, Janice. *Janice VanCleave's Biology for Every Kid.* New York: Wiley, 1990.

———. *Janice VanCleave's The Human Body for Every Kid.* New York: Wiley, 1995.

Walker, Richard. *The Children's Atlas of the Human Body.* Brookfield, Conn.: Millbrook Press, 1994.

Weiner, Esther. *The Incredible Human Body.* New York: Scholastic, 1996.

Wiese, Jim. *Head to Toe Science.* New York: Wiley, 2000.

Inhale, Exhale

So You Want to Do a Project about **Lung Capacity!**

Let's Explore

Purpose

To measure the lungs' air capacity.

Materials

masking tape
1-gallon (4-L) hard plastic or glass jug with lid
1-cup (250-mL) measuring cup
water
marking pen
blue food coloring
large plastic dishpan
2-foot (60-cm) piece of aquarium tubing
drinking straw
helper

Procedure

1. Place a strip of masking tape down the side of the jug.
2. Use the measuring cup to add 16 cups (4 L) of water to the jug, 1 cup (250 mL) at a time. Use the marking pen to mark a line on the tape to indicate the level after each cup of water.
3. Add 20 or more drops of food coloring to the water. Secure the lid on the jug, then shake the jug to mix the water and food coloring.
4. Fill the dishpan about half full with water.
5. Place the jug upside down in the dishpan and remove the lid.
6. Ask your helper to hold the jug. Do not allow air bubbles to enter the jug.
7. Place about 4 inches (10 cm) of one end of the tubing into the mouth of the jug.
8. Insert the drinking straw into the free end of the tubing to make a sanitary mouthpiece.

9. Take a normal breath and **exhale** (breathe out) through the straw into the tubing.
10. Use the scale on the jug to determine the **volume** (amount of occupied space) of your exhaled breath in cups. Estimate the volume between marks to the nearest one-fourth cup (0.63 mL). Record this measurement as tidal air in a Lung Capacity Data table like the one shown.
11. Empty the jug and pan and repeat steps 3 to 8.
12. Inhale normally and exhale through the straw into the tubing, making an effort to force all the air from your lungs. Record this measurement as tidal air plus reserve air. Subtract the tidal air volume and record the results as reserve air.
13. Repeat step 11, then inhale deeply and force all the air you can from your lungs. Record this measurement as **vital capacity** (maximum volume of air that can be inhaled or exhaled during forced breathing). Vital capacity is the tidal air plus reserve air plus **complemental air** (the volume of air that can be inhaled with force).
14. Subtract the reserve air from the vital capacity to calculate complemental air, then enter your results in the data table.

44

Results

LUNG CAPACITY DATA

Lung Capacity	Measurement
Tidal air	1¾ cups (437 mL)
Tidal air + reserve air	7²⁄₄ cups (1,875 mL)
Reserve air	5¾ cups (1,438 mL)
Complemental air	7¼ cups (1,812 mL)
Total vital capacity	14¾ cups (3,687 mL)

Why?

When the lungs are filled, they hold varying volumes of air depending on the size of the person. The author's lungs hold about 14¾ cups (3,687 mL). About 5¾ cups (1,438 mL) of this amount is tidal air. **Tidal air** is the volume of air involved during normal, relaxed **inspiration** (breathing in) and **expiration** (breathing out). The volume of air that can be forced out after normal expiration is called **reserve air,** and the volume of air that can be inhaled with force is called complemental air. With vigorous inspiration and expiration, the tidal air plus reserve air plus complemental air (or total vital capacity) can be expelled. Even with maximum expiration, the lungs are not empty. For adults, depending on size, there is always about 4 cups (1 L) of air that remains in the lungs, and this volume is referred to as **residual air.**

FOR FURTHER INVESTIGATION

A child is smaller than an adult. Does an adult have a greater lung capacity than a child? A project question might be, How does body size affect the lungs' vital capacity?

Clues for Your Investigation

1. Ask people of different body sizes to repeat the experiment. You need to decide how you want to measure body size: Weight? Height? Chest measurement?

2. The experiment should be repeated by each person four or more times. A rest period of 10 or more minutes can be given between tests, but whatever the procedure, use the same procedure for each person taking the test. Average the results for each person.
3. A graph comparing the measured body size and vital capacity can be made and displayed.

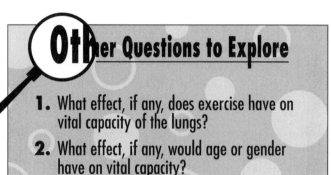

Other Questions to Explore

1. What effect, if any, does exercise have on vital capacity of the lungs?
2. What effect, if any, would age or gender have on vital capacity?

REFERENCES AND PROJECT BOOKS

Allison, Linda. *Blood and Guts.* New York: Little, Brown, 1976.

Beckelman, Laurie. *The Human Body.* Pleasantville, N.Y.: Reader's Digest, 1999.

Chisholm, Jane. *Introduction to Biology.* London: Usborne, 1984.

Parker, Steve. *The Human Body.* Brookfield, Conn.: Copper Beech Books, 1995.

———. *The Lungs and Breathing.* New York: Franklin Watts, 1991.

Saunderson, Jane. *Heart and Lungs.* New York: Troll, 1992.

VanCleave, Janice. *Janice VanCleave's Animals.* New York: Wiley, 1992.

———. *Janice VanCleave's A+ Projects in Biology.* New York: Wiley, 1993.

———. *Janice VanCleave's Biology for Every Kid.* New York: Wiley, 1990.

Weiner, Esther. *The Incredible Human Body.* New York: Scholastic, 1996.

Wiese, Jim. *Head to Toe Science.* New York: Wiley, 2000.

Chemistry

21 Changes

So You Want to Do a Project about **Phases of Matter!**

LET'S EXPLORE

Purpose

To determine the physical properties of the phases of matter.

Materials

marker
3 resealable sandwich bags
tap water
ice cube
drinking straw
3 small paper or plastic bowls

Procedure

1. Use the marker to label one of the bags "Liquid," the second bag "Solid," and the third bag "Gas."
2. Fill the Liquid bag about half full with water and seal the bag.
3. Place the ice cube in the Solid bag and seal.
4. Insert the straw into the Gas bag and close the bag as much as possible around the straw.
5. Blow through the straw to inflate the bag. Then remove the straw and immediately seal the bag.
6. Place all three bags on a table.
7. Observe the contents of the Liquid bag. Then pour the contents of the bag into one of the bowls, and observe the contents of the bowl.
8. Repeat step 7 with the Solid bag and then with the Gas bag.

Results

The ice stays the same shape when poured into the bowl, but the water spreads out. The gas is invisible.

Why?

Matter is anything that has **mass** (amount of material) and volume (takes up space). The three common **phases** (forms) of matter are solid, liquid, and gas. **Solids** have a definite shape and volume. The ice was the same shape and volume in the bowl as in the bag. **Liquids** have no definite shape but have a definite volume. The liquid water spread out in the bowl, but the amount of water was the same in the bowl as in the bag. **Gases,** such as the gas exhaled from your body, have no definite shape or volume. When confined in a container, such as a closed plastic bag, the gas had the volume of the bag. But when the bag was opened, the gas began to **diffuse** (spread freely) through the air in the room.

FOR FURTHER INVESTIGATION

An **atom** is a building block of matter. When two or more atoms are connected by a **bond** (force that links atoms together), a **molecule** is formed. In liquid water, the molecules are **bonded** (attached) to each other, forming short chains. These chains are flexible. In ice, six water molecules bond together to form a stiff **hexagonal** (six-sided) **crystal** (a solid that has its atoms arranged in a definite geometric shape). All the hexagonal ice crystals bond together, forming one large block of ice. Which do you think has a greater volume—liquid water or the same amount of water after it freezes? A project question might be, Given an equal number of molecules, how does the volume of ice compare to that of liquid water?

Clues for Your Investigation

Discover how the volumes of ice and liquid water compare by following these steps:

1. Fill a plastic container to overflowing with water. Secure the lid, then observe any bulging of the lid.
2. Take a photograph of the side of the container showing any bulge in the lid.

3. Place the container in a freezer until the water freezes. This might take 6 or more hours. Observe the lid for bulging.
4. Take a second photograph to document any bulging of the lid after freezing.

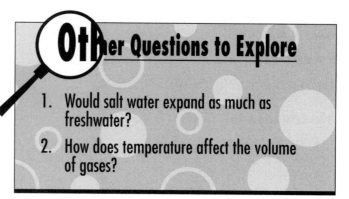

Other Questions to Explore

1. Would salt water expand as much as freshwater?
2. How does temperature affect the volume of gases?

REFERENCES AND PROJECT BOOKS

Churchill, E. Richard. *365 Simple Science Experiments with Everyday Materials.* New York: Black Dog & Leventhal, 1997.

Doherty, Paul, and Don Rathjen. *The Cool Hot Rod and Other Electrifying Experiments on Energy and Matter.* New York: Wiley, 1991.

Edom, Helen. *Science with Water.* London: Usborne, 1990.

Reader's Digest. *Did You Know?* Pleasantville, N.Y.: Reader's Digest, 1990.

Smith, Alastair, ed. *The Usborne Big Book of Experiments.* London: Usborne, 1996.

VanCleave, Janice. *Janice VanCleave's Chemistry for Every Kid.* New York: Wiley, 1989.

LET'S EXPLORE

Purpose

To demonstrate a chemical change.

Materials

Polident tablet
10-ounce (300-mL) clear plastic drinking cup
tap water

Procedure

1. Observe the appearance of the dry tablet. Record your observation in a Chemical Change Data table like the one shown.
2. Fill the cup about half full with water.
3. Drop the tablet in the water. Observe and record the results.
4. Continue to observe and record the descriptions of the contents of the cup until there is no further change.

CHEMICAL CHANGE DATA

	Dry Tablet	Tablet + Water
Polident Tablet		

Results

The tablet is green and solid when dry. When added to water, it vigorously produces bubbles for a time. Then the tablet appears to have disappeared, leaving a foamy green liquid.

Why?

The solid tablet combines with liquid water to form at least one new substance, a gas, as indicated by the bubbles. A process by which one or more substances, called **reactants,** are changed into one or more different substances, called **products,** is called a **chemical reaction** or **chemical change.**

In order for a chemical reaction to occur, the molecules of water must combine with the molecules on the surface of the tablet. This combination occurs because all particles of matter, such as the tablet and the water, have **kinetic energy** (energy of motion). This means the particles are in motion. In solids the motion is more of a **vibration** (back-and-forth motion) around a center point, but in liquids the particles can move from one place to another. The motion of the water molecules causes random collisions with the tablet, resulting in a combination of the water molecules and molecules on the surface of the antacid tablet.

FOR FURTHER INVESTIGATION

An increase of temperature is an indication of an increase of kinetic energy of a substance. Would the tablet disappear faster in hot water? A project question might be, How does temperature affect the speed of a chemical reaction?

Clues for Your Investigation

1. Repeat the investigation using different water temperatures. Cold water can be made by adding ice cubes to tap water. Remove the ice cubes before adding the tablet. Cool water is tap water at room temperature. Hot water can be obtained from the tap. Repeat the experiment four or more times at the same temperatures. *CAUTION: Ask an adult to fill the cups with hot water and to supervise handling of the cups of hot water.*

2. To measure the rate of the reaction, test one set of cups at a time, starting with the four cups of cold water. Observe the tablets and record the time the tablets are dropped in the water and the time each stops bubbling. Average this time. Repeat, testing the other two sets of cups (four cups of cool water and four cups of hot water) one at a time. Record your results in a Chemical Reaction Time Data table like the one shown.

CHEMICAL REACTION TIME DATA

Temperature	Time				
	Test 1	Test 2	Test 3	Test 4	Average
Cold Water					
Cool Water					
Hot Water					

Other Questions to Explore

1. How does the concentration of the reactants affect the speed of a chemical reaction?
2. Would the brand of tablet used in the original experiment affect the speed of the chemical reaction?

REFERENCES AND PROJECT BOOKS

Churchill, E. Richard. *365 Simple Science Experiments with Everyday Materials.* New York: Black Dog & Leventhal, 1997.

Heiserman, David L. *Exploring Chemical Elements and Their Compounds.* Blue Ridge Summit, Pa.: Tab Books, 1992.

Kenda, Margaret, and Phyllis S. Williams. *Science Wizardry for Kids.* Hauppauge, N.Y.: Barron's, 1992.

Kerrod, Robin. *Simon & Schuster Young Readers' Book of Science.* New York: Simon & Schuster, 1991.

Nye, Bill. *Bill Nye the Science Guy's Big Blast of Science.* Reading, Mass.: Addison-Wesley, 1993.

Strauss, Michael. *Where Puddles Go.* Portsmouth, N.H.: Heinemann, 1995.

VanCleave, Janice. *Janice VanCleave's Chemistry for Every Kid.* New York: Wiley, 1989.

Wiese, Jim. *Rocket Science.* New York: Wiley, 1995.

23 Glob

So You Want to Do a Project about **Polymers!**

LET'S EXPLORE

Purpose

To make a polymer.

Materials

masking tape
marker
two 1-pint (500-mL) jars
4-ounce (120-mL) bottle of white multipurpose
    school glue
tap water
2 mixing spoons
1 teaspoon (5 mL) borax powder (found near
    laundry detergents in the supermarket)
1-cup (250-mL) measuring cup
two 3-ounce (90-mL) paper cups
2-quart (2-L) bowl
12-inch (30-cm) -square piece of waxed paper
timer

Procedure

*CAUTION: As with any chemistry experiment,
follow warnings on the containers of the materials used. Do not eat the glob produced.*

1. Use the masking tape and marker to label
   the jars "Borax" and "Glue."
2. Pour the glue into the Glue jar.
3. Fill the empty glue bottle with water and
   pour the water into the Glue jar. Stir the
   glue and water to mix them together
   thoroughly.
4. Put the borax and 1 cup (250 mL) of water
   into the Borax jar. Stir, using a different
   spoon, until the borax dissolves.
5. Fill the paper cups, one with the glue-and-
   water mixture and the other with the
   borax-and-water mixture.

6. Pour the contents of each paper cup into
   the bowl, using either spoon to stir the mixture until it thickens.

7. Take the thickened substance called glob
   that forms out of the bowl and place it on
   the waxed paper for 1 to 2 minutes. Then
   remove the glob from the paper and knead
   it with your hands for about 1 minute.
8. Try these experiments with the glob and
   record your observations of how the glob
   responds in a data table:

   ● Roll the glob into a ball and bounce it on
     a smooth surface.

   ● Hold it in your hands and quickly pull
     the ends in opposite directions.

   ● Hold it in your hands and very slowly
     pull the ends in opposite directions.

Results

You have made a soft, **pliable** (easily bent) material that spreads out when not confined, bounces slightly when dropped, breaks apart if pulled quickly, and stretches if pulled slowly.

Why?

In this experiment, a chemical reaction occurs when the reactants—borax, glue, and water—combine to form a cross-linked polymer called a glob. **Cross-links** are chemical bridges between two molecules. A **polymer** is a large, chainlike molecule made by combining many small single molecules called **monomers.** In this experiment, the borax forms bridges (cross-links) between the polymer chains in the glue much as the rungs of a ladder link the two sides together. The cross-linked polymer produced is much more **viscous** (thick; having a high resistance to flow) than the glue.

The glob has some properties of a solid—for example, it breaks when pressure is applied—and some properties of a liquid—for example, it flows. Sir Isaac Newton (1642–1727), an English scientist, described **fluids** (liquid or gas) as materials that flow under pressure. Since the glob flows, it is a fluid. But unlike the fluids described by Newton, the glob has some properties of a solid, so it is called a **non-Newtonian fluid.**

FOR FURTHER INVESTIGATION

The cross-links make the glob less fluid than glue. Would more cross-links make the glob solid? A project question might be, How would the concentration of the reactants affect the fluid property of the glob?

Clues for Your Investigation

CAUTION: *Do not change the concentrations of materials in chemical reactions unless you know that it is safe, such as in this investigation.*

1. Make three different mixtures of borax and water and label the three jars "A," "B," and "C." Jar A will contain the original borax mixture, jar B will contain half the amount of borax in the original mixture, and jar C will contain two times the amount of borax in the original mixture.
2. Using the borax mixture in each of the jars—A, B, and C—repeat the original investigation using the original glue mixture.

Other Questions to Explore

1. Would changing the concentration of the glue affect the results?
2. How would temperature affect the fluid property of the glob?

REFERENCES AND PROJECT BOOKS

Branzei, Sylvia. *Grossology.* Reading, Mass.: Addison-Wesley, 1995.

Levine, Shar, and Allison Grafton. *Einstein's Science Parties: Easy Parties for Curious Kids.* New York: Wiley, 1994.

Marks, Diana F. *Glues, Brews, and Goos: Recipes and Formulas for Almost Any Classroom Project.* Englewood, Colo.: Teacher Ideas Press, 1996.

Potter, Jean. *Science in Seconds with Toys.* New York: Wiley, 1998.

Soucie, Gary. *What's the Difference between Lenses and Prisms and Other Scientific Things?* New York: Wiley, 1995.

VanCleave, Janice. *Janice VanCleave's 200 Gooey, Slippery, Slimy, Weird, and Fun Experiments.* New York: Wiley, 1993.

Wellnitz, William R. *Homemade Slime and Rubber Bones!* Blue Ridge Summit, Pa.: Tab Books, 1993.

LET'S EXPLORE

Purpose

To measure the absorbency of a paper towel.

Materials

scissors
1-inch (2.5-cm) -wide masking tape
10-ounce (300-mL) plastic cup
walnut-size piece of modeling clay
pencil
tap water
marker
4 identical 2-ply paper towels with as flat a
    texture as possible
timer
metric ruler

Procedure

1. Cut a piece of masking tape the same length as the height of the cup. Place this tape down the side of the cup.
2. Divide the clay in half and use the two pieces to secure the pencil across the top of the cup.
3. Fill the cup about half full with water and, using the marker, mark the water level on the tape. Label the mark 0.
4. Take one of the paper towels, place the short sides together, and fold the paper towel in half three times in the same direction, producing a long, narrow, eight-ply strip.
5. Fold the resulting strip in half, placing the short sides together. Crease the folded edge.
6. Place the strip of paper towel over the pencil on the cup of water so that the fold rests on top of the pencil and the ends touch the bottom of the cup.

7. Leave the paper towel in the water for 10 seconds, then raise it above the water and allow the water to drip from the paper towel for 10 seconds. Discard the wet paper towel.
8. Mark a small line across the tape even with the new water level. Label this line 1.
9. Measure the distance from the zero mark to line 1 in millimeters. Record this number as the water absorbency number for test 1 in an Absorbency Data table like the one shown.

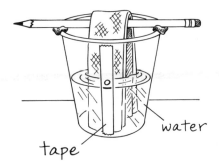
water
tape

10. Repeat steps 3 to 8 three times, using the remaining paper towels and refilling the cup with water to the zero mark for each test. Number the lines 2 to 4.
11. Repeat step 9 for test lines 2 to 4.
12. Average the absorbency numbers by adding the amounts absorbed in each of the four tests and dividing the sum by 4. Record the average in your data table.

Results

The absorbency number of a brand of paper towels is determined

Why?

In this investigation, the term **absorption** is used to mean the soaking up of a liquid by a solid. The liquid is water, and the solid is the

ABSORBENCY DATA

	Test 1	Test 2	Test 3	Test 4	Average
Absorbency number					

paper towel. Absorption by the paper towel is the result of the attraction between the water molecules and the attraction of the water molecules to the paper towel. The attraction between like molecules (water) is called **cohesion,** and the attraction between unlike molecules (water and paper towel) is called **adhesion.** In this investigation, there is cohesion between the water molecules and adhesion between the water molecules and the molecules in the paper towel. Because water molecules are more attracted to the paper towel than to each other, the water is absorbed, causing the paper towel to be wet.

The water moves through the paper towel because of capillarity. **Capillarity** is the tendency of liquids to rise or move through small tubes or openings of porous material, such as paper towels. The paper towel is made of tiny fibers that lie together, forming short, narrow spaces that act as tiny tubes. Water is attracted to the fibers, causing the water to move through the tubelike spaces in the paper towel. The greater the attraction between the water and the fibers, the greater the absorbency.

The **absorbency number** determined in this investigation is not a measurement of the volume of water absorbed. Instead, it is a number that can be used to compare the absorbency of different paper towels as long as the same measuring instrument is used.

FOR FURTHER INVESTIGATION

Some paper towels are rougher in texture than others. Does a rough paper towel absorb more water than a smooth one? A project question might be, How does the texture of paper towels affect absorbency?

Clues for Your Investigation

1. Repeat the experiment, using paper towels with different textures.
2. Make sure the paper towels are the same size and the same ply. If necessary, cut the towels to a specific size, such as 10 inches (25 cm) square.
3. If possible, use white paper towels without colored designs.

Other Questions to Explore

1. How could the volume of water absorbed by each paper towel be determined?
2. How does color affect paper towels' absorbency?
3. How does density of paper towels affect their absorbency?
4. How high above the water line will water move in paper towels?
5. Do dissolved materials, such as salt, in water affect absorbency of paper towels?

REFERENCES AND PROJECT BOOKS

Churchill, E. Richard. *365 Simple Science Experiments with Everyday Materials.* New York: Black Dog & Leventhal, 1997.

Hann, Judith. *How Science Works.* Pleasantville, N.Y.: Reader's Digest, 1991.

Nye, Bill. *Bill Nye the Science Guy's Consider the Following.* New York: Scholastic, 1995.

Reader's Digest. *Why in the World?* Pleasantville, N.Y.: Reader's Digest, 1994.

VanCleave, Janice. *Janice VanCleave's Chemistry for Every Kid.* New York: Wiley, 1989.

25 Riser

So You Want to Do a Project about **Specific Gravity!**

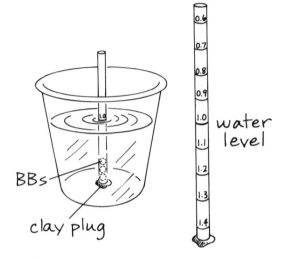

water level

BBs

clay plug

Let's Explore

Purpose

To construct a hydrometer.

Materials

10-ounce (300-mL) plastic cup
tap water
scissors
drinking straw
grape-size piece of modeling clay
5 BBs
fine-point permanent black marking pen
metric ruler

Procedure

1. Fill the cup about three-fourths full with water.
2. Cut a 4-inch (10-cm) section from the straw.
3. Plug one end of the piece of straw with clay.
4. Drop three of the BBs into the straw. Then try to stand the straw, clay plug down, in the cup of water. You want the straw to stand upright in the water with about half of the straw above the water line. If the straw does not stand upright and/or is not halfway above the water line, add one BB at a time until it is.
5. With the marking pen, draw a line on the straw even with the water line.
6. Remove the BB-filled straw from the water. Label the line 1.0.
7. Using the ruler and marker, start at the line on the straw and mark as many lines as possible 1 cm apart toward the clay end of the straw. Number these 1.1, 1.2, and so on.
8. Repeat step 7, making lines toward the open end of the straw. Number these 0.9, 0.8, and so on.

Results

You have made a hydrometer.

Why?

A **hydrometer** is an instrument used to compare the **density** (mass per unit volume) of a liquid substance to the density of pure water. This comparison of densities is called **specific gravity.** The scale on the hydrometer in this investigation is a model of how a hydrometer works and cannot be used to measure actual specific gravity. Starting at 1.0 at the water line, this is the height of the hydrometer in any liquid having the same density as that of the tap water used. The other marks on the scale indicate a relative increase or decrease in specific gravity. The lower the hydrometer sinks in a liquid, the lower its specific gravity. Thus, scale readings less than 1.0 mean the liquid's density is less than the density of water. The higher the hydrometer rises in the liquid, the greater the liquid's specific gravity, indicated by scale readings greater than 1.0.

FOR FURTHER INVESTIGATION

Ocean water is salty. Is salt water denser than freshwater? A project question might be, How does the **salinity** (salt concentration) of water affect its specific gravity?

Clues for Your Investigation

1. Using the hydrometer made in the original experiment, determine the density of different salt solutions. Make the salt solutions with equal amounts of water but different amounts of salt, such as the solutions shown here in the Specific Gravity Data table. *NOTE: Since the hydrometer was made using tap water, tap water must also be used in the test solutions.* You may wish to repeat the original experiment using distilled water so that it indicates the density of pure water and not tap water that has some dissolved materials in it. Measure and keep a record of how much salt you put into each cup.

2. For each cup of liquid, take four or more readings with the hydrometer and average them. For each reading, place the hydrometer in the liquid and allow it and the water to become still. Then read and record where the water line touches the mark on the hydrometer in a Specific Gravity Data

table like the one shown. Estimate measurements between marks. For example, 1.25 would be halfway between marks 1.2 and 1.3. Average the test results of each liquid.

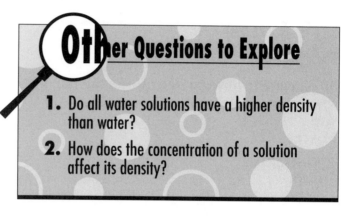

Other Questions to Explore

1. Do all water solutions have a higher density than water?

2. How does the concentration of a solution affect its density?

REFERENCES AND PROJECT BOOKS

Churchill, E. Richard. *365 Simple Science Experiments with Everyday Materials.* New York: Black Dog & Leventhal, 1997.

Edom, Helen. *Science with Water.* London: Usborne, 1992.

Gibson, Gary. *Science for Fun Experiments.* Brookfield, Conn.: Copper Beech Books, 1996.

VanCleave, Janice. *Janice VanCleave's A+ Projects in Chemistry.* New York: Wiley, 1993.

———. *Janice VanCleave's Chemistry for Every Kid.* New York: Wiley, 1989.

Walpole, Brenda. *175 Science Experiments to Amuse and Amaze Your Friends.* New York: Random House, 1988.

SPECIFIC GRAVITY DATA

Test	Salt Solution	Hydrometer Reading				
		Test 1	Test 2	Test 3	Test 4	Average
A	1 cup (250 mL) tap water					
B	1 cup (250 mL) tap water + 1 teaspoon (5 mL) salt					
C	1 cup (250 mL) tap water + 2 teaspoons (10 mL) salt					
D	1 cup (250 mL) tap water + 3 teaspoons (15 mL) salt					
E	1 cup (250 mL) tap water + 4 teaspoons (20 mL) salt					

LET'S EXPLORE

Purpose

To determine how stirring affects the rate at which materials dissolve in a solution.

Materials

masking tape
marker
two 10-ounce (300-mL) transparent plastic cups
1-cup (250-mL) measuring cup
tap water
2 sugar cubes
timer
spoon

Procedure

1. Use the tape and marker to label the two cups "A" and "B."
2. Pour ½ cup (125 mL) of water into each plastic cup.
3. Add one sugar cube to each cup of water. Start the timer.
4. Using the spoon, gently stir the water in cup A until the sugar cube has completely dissolved and is no longer visible. Record the time as test 1 for cup A in a Dissolving Time Data table like the one shown.

STATIC ELECTRICITY DATA

Cup	Time				
---	Test 1	Test 2	Test 3	Test 4	Average
A					
B					

5. Continue to let the timer run and observe cup B but do not stir the water.

6. When the sugar cube is completely dissolved so that no sugar is visible, record the time as test 1 for cup B.
7. Repeat steps 2 through 6 three or more times and average the results.

Results

The sugar cube that is stirred (in cup A) dissolves faster.

Why?

A solution is a **homogenous mixture** (a combination of two or more substances that is the same throughout). A solution is made of two parts: a solute that dissolves, meaning it breaks up into small particles—molecules or atoms—and moves throughout the second part, called the solvent. In this investigation, sugar is the solute and water the solvent. When the sugar is added to the water, it dissolves to form a solution. The dissolving of the sugar occurs because water molecules randomly move about, colliding with the surface of the sugar. While the cohesion (attraction between like molecules) between the molecules of the sugar is great enough to hold them together, the adhesion (attraction between unlike molecules) between the water molecules and sugar molecules is great enough to pull the sugar molecules off the sugar cube's surface. Because of the attraction of water molecules for the sugar molecules, each of the freed sugar molecules becomes completely surrounded by water molecules. This dissolving process by which water molecules surround a solute molecule is called **hydration** or **solvation.**

The rate of hydration can be increased by stirring. Stirring the mixture aids in the dissolving of the solute particles by moving hydrated solute particles away and bringing fresh portions of the solvent (water) in contact with the undissolved solute (sugar).

FOR FURTHER INVESTIGATION

As the temperature of a liquid increases, the motion of its molecules also increases. Would sugar dissolve faster in hot water? A project question might be, What effect does temperature have on the dissolving rate of sugar?

Clues for Your Investigation

Repeat the original investigation with water at three different temperatures—hot, cool, and cold—but don't stir any of the cups. "Hot" can be hot tap water, "cool" can be water at room temperature, and "cold" can be tap water to which ice has been added to reduce the temperature. (Remove the ice before adding the

sugar.) *CAUTION: Ask an adult to fill the cups with hot water and to supervise handling of the cups of hot water.*

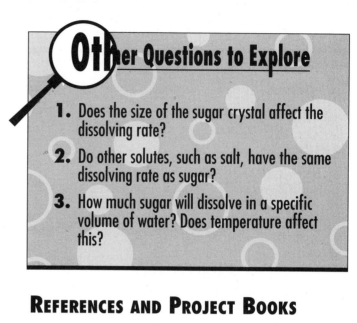

Other Questions to Explore

1. Does the size of the sugar crystal affect the dissolving rate?

2. Do other solutes, such as salt, have the same dissolving rate as sugar?

3. How much sugar will dissolve in a specific volume of water? Does temperature affect this?

REFERENCES AND PROJECT BOOKS

Churchill, E. Richard. *365 Simple Science Experiments with Everyday Materials.* New York: Black Dog & Leventhal, 1997.

Gibson, Gary. *Science for Fun Experiments.* Brookfield, Conn.: Copper Beech Books, 1996.

Kenda, Margaret, and Phyllis S. Williams. *Science Wizardry for Kids.* Hauppauge, N.Y.: Barron's, 1992.

Nye, Bill. *Bill Nye the Science Guy's Big Blast of Science.* Reading, Mass.: Addison-Wesley, 1993.

Strauss, Michael. *Where Puddles Go.* Portsmouth, N.H.: Heinemann, 1995.

VanCleave, Janice A. *Janice VanCleave's A+ Projects in Chemistry.* New York: Wiley, 1993.

———. *Janice VanCleave's Chemistry for Every Kid.* New York: Wiley, 1989.

27 Separator

So You Want to Do a Project about **Chromatography!**

LET'S EXPLORE

Purpose

To separate the parts of ink.

Materials

10-ounce (300-mL) plastic cup
3¼-by-2⅜-inch (8.1-by-5.9-cm) basket-type
  coffee filter
coin (quarter)
green water-soluble marker
3-ounce (90-mL) paper cup
tap water

Procedure

1. Set the plastic cup open side up on a table and stretch the filter over the mouth of the cup. Squeeze the filter around the sides of the cup to hold the filter in place.
2. Place the coin in the center of the filter and, with the marker, draw a circle on the filter by tracing around the coin.
3. Fill the paper cup with water.
4. Dip your finger in the water, then touch the center of the circle with your wet fingertip. Watch the wet spot on the filter until no changes are seen.
5. If there are any dry areas in the circle drawn on the filter, repeat step 6.

Results

When water is added, the green ink begins to separate into different colors. Depending on the ink used, varying amounts of blue and yellow can be seen.

Why?

Ink is a mixture of a fast-drying liquid and **pigments** (substances that give a material

water

color). The pigment in the dried ink on the paper dissolves in the water added to the paper. This watery mixture is absorbed by and moves through the paper. The different colored pigments have different amounts of attraction to the filter paper. The pigment with the least attraction will move a greater distance through the paper. Generally, blue pigment in ink moves farthest, followed by yellow. This method of separating parts of a mixture is called **chromatography.**

FOR FURTHER INVESTIGATION

Mixing different pigments produces different colors. What pigments are in black ink? Do you think all black inks are made of the same pigments? A project question might be, How do the pigments in different brands of water-soluble black ink compare?

Clues for Your Investigation

1. Repeat the investigation with different brands of black water-soluble ink. Write the name of each brand on the filter paper.
2. Display the markers and the filter paper with your written conclusion of the results.

Other Questions to Explore

1. What pigments are in other colors of ink?
2. Would different kinds of paper produce the same results?

REFERENCES AND PROJECT BOOKS

Ardley, Neil. *The Science Book of Color.* New York: Gulliver Books, 1991.

Churchill, E. Richard. *365 Simple Science Experiments with Everyday Materials.* New York: Black Dog & Leventhal, 1997.

Johnson, Mary. *Chemistry Experiments.* London: Usborne, 1981.

Lantier-Sampon, Patricia, ed. *Smithsonian Institution: Color and Light.* Milwaukee: Gareth Stevens, 1993.

Murphy, Pat, Ellen Klages, and Linda Shore. *The Science Explorer.* New York: Owl Books, 1996.

Potter, Jean. *Science in Seconds with Toys.* New York: Wiley, 1998.

VanCleave, Janice. *Janice VanCleave's Chemistry for Every Kid.* New York: Wiley, 1989.

28 Meltdown!

So You Want to Do a Project about **Ice!**

Let's Explore

Purpose

To demonstrate the effect of salt on ice.

Materials

tape
marker
2 saucers
2 ice cubes
½ teaspoon (2.5 mL) salt
timer

Procedure

1. Use the tape and marker to label one of the saucers "Salt" and the other "No Salt."
2. Place one ice cube in each saucer.
3. Place the salt on the ice in the Salt saucer.
4. Place both saucers in a freezer.
5. Observe the contents of the saucer every 10 minutes for 30 or more minutes.

Results

The ice covered with salt begins to melt.

Why?

When salt and water are mixed together, the salt dissolves, which means the salt breaks into small particles that thoroughly mix with the water. A solution made with a liquid solvent is called a **liquid solution.** The temperature at which a liquid **freezes** (changes to a solid) is called the **freezing point.** A liquid solution of salt water has a lower freezing point than water alone. The greater the concentration of the salt solution, the lower its freezing point.

At or just below freezing temperatures, ice is said to have a "wet" slippery surface. But at temperatures well below freezing, ice has a "dry" surface and is barely slippery. This is because as the ice gets colder, the surface molecules are bound together more tightly. So when salt is sprinkled on the surface of "wet" ice, the salt dissolves in the more loosely bound molecules on the surface layer of the ice and lowers the freezing point of the water on the surface. Even though the solution is at or slightly below the freezing point of water, the salt water does not refreeze. At very low temperatures, it is difficult to melt ice with salt because the ice has a dry surface and salt cannot dissolve in the tightly bound surface water molecules. So the ice doesn't melt.

The ice cube in the No Salt saucer is called a control. A **control** is a test in which all of the variables (things that can have an effect on the results of an experiment, such as containers, light, and heat) are the same except one. In this experiment, salt is the variable that is different. By omitting salt from the control, it can be determined if salt is the variable that causes the ice to melt.

FOR FURTHER INVESTIGATION

In wintertime, both salt and sand are used to keep cars from slipping on icy roads and people from slipping on icy sidewalks. Salt applied to an icy sidewalk will melt the ice, but the salt may damage plants along the sidewalk. This is why sand is often used. Sand increases friction, but does sand melt ice? A project question might be, What effect does sand have on the melting of ice?

Clues for Your Investigation

1. Repeat the investigation, using salt on some ice cubes and sand on others. Use equal amounts of sand and salt with equal amounts of ice.
2. Record the appearance of the ice in each sample after specific time intervals. Photographs of the ice cubes could be taken to represent the results.

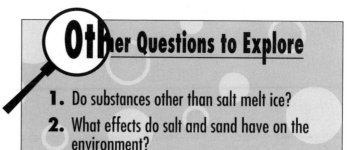

1. Do substances other than salt melt ice?
2. What effects do salt and sand have on the environment?

REFERENCES AND PROJECT BOOKS

Churchill, E. Richard. *365 Simple Science Experiments with Everyday Materials.* New York: Black Dog & Leventhal, 1997.

Reader's Digest. *Why in the World?* Pleasantville, N.Y.: Reader's Digest, 1994.

Smith, Alastair, ed. *The Usborne Big Book of Experiments.* London: Usborne, 1996.

VanCleave, Janice. *Janice VanCleave's Chemistry for Every Kid.* New York: Wiley, 1989.

————. *Science around the Year.* New York: Wiley, 2000.

29 Cleanup!

So You Want to Do a Project about **Emulsifiers!**

LET'S EXPLORE

Purpose

To determine the effect of detergent on an oil-and-water mixture.

Materials

masking tape
pen
2 empty 20-ounce (600-mL) water bottles with caps
tap water
1 teaspoon (5 mL) liquid cooking oil
½-teaspoon (2.5-mL) measuring spoon
1 teaspoon (5 mL) dishwashing liquid

Procedure

1. Use the tape and pen to label the bottles "A" and "B."
2. Fill bottle A about three-fourths full with water and add ½ teaspoon (2.5 mL) of oil to the bottle of water.
3. Repeat step 2 with bottle B.
4. Add the dishwashing liquid to bottle B, and then seal each bottle with its cap.
5. Shake each bottle 20 times, and then allow both bottles to stand for 3 minutes.
6. Observe the contents of each bottle.

Results

At first the oil and water in each bottle mixed. After standing, the contents of bottle A separated into two layers, while the contents of bottle B remained mixed.

Why?

It is commonly said that oil and water do not mix. When oil and water are put in the same container and stirred or shaken, the oil breaks

up into globules. This combination of two or more substances that is not the same throughout is called a **heterogeneous mixture.** After standing, the oil and water separate into two layers. Dishwashing liquid is a **detergent** (a chemical that cleans, especially if it removes oily dirt). Detergent molecules are **emulsifiers,** which means they cause oil and water not to separate. In this investigation, the detergent keeps the oil suspended in small globules in the water. This occurs because the detergent molecules have two ends, one end that **repels** (pushes away) oil but attracts water and an opposite end that repels water but attracts oil.

Shaking the bottles causes some of the oil to break into microscopic globules. In bottle B, the detergent molecules cover the oil globules by embedding their oil-attracting ends in the oil globules. Their water-attracting ends stick out and have a negative charge. Since like charges repel each other, the negatively charged ends of the detergent molecules that cover the oil globules repel each other. The oil globules stay suspended in the water. In bottle A, the oil globules **coalesce** (join together) and float to the top of the bottle.

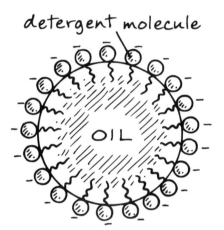

detergent molecule

OIL

FOR FURTHER INVESTIGATION

There are different kinds of dishwashing liquids. Which cleans oily dishes better—thick or thin dishwashing liquid? A project question might be, What effect, if any, does the **viscosity** (measure of thickness) of detergent have on how it emulsifies?

Clues for Your Investigation

1. Repeat the investigation with detergents of different viscosities.
2. To measure the viscosity of a detergent, put a drop of dishwashing liquid on one end of a metal baking sheet. Raise this end of the pan about 45° and watch the drop move down the pan. Rate the viscosity of

each detergent by how fast the drops flow down the pan, with the most viscous detergent being the one with the slowest-moving drops.
3. To rate the emulsifying ability of each detergent, add ½ teaspoon (2.5 mL) of oil to the bottle at a time. Continue adding oil until no more oil mixes with the water. When the additional oil no longer mixes with the water, do not include that amount of oil in your total.

Other Questions to Explore

1. Is a dish detergent as effective in cleaning oil from cloth as a laundry detergent?
2. Is an oil (liquid) harder to clean than a fat (solid)?

REFERENCES AND PROJECT BOOKS

Churchill, E. Richard. *365 Simple Science Experiments with Everyday Materials.* New York: Black Dog & Leventhal, 1997.

Potter, Jean. *Nature in a Nutshell for Kids.* New York: Wiley, 1995.

Reader's Digest. *Why in the World?* Pleasantville, N.Y.: Reader's Digest, 1994.

Soucie, Gary. *What's the Difference between Lenses and Prisms and Other Scientific Things?* New York: Wiley, 1995.

VanCleave, Janice. *Janice VanCleave's Food and Nutrition for Every Kid.* New York: Wiley, 1999.

———. *Janice VanCleave's Molecules.* New York: Wiley, 1993.

Wellnitz, William R. *Homemade Slime and Rubber Bones!* Blue Ridge Summit, Pa.: Tab Books, 1993.

30 Brown Banana

So You Want to Do a Project about **Oxidation!**

LET'S EXPLORE

Purpose

To determine if vitamin C can inhibit oxidation.

Materials

banana
dinner knife
2 saucers
2 sheets of white copy paper
pen
3 vitamin C tablets (100-mg work well)
cutting board
rolling pin
timer

Procedure

1. Peel the banana, and then slice it into eight pieces.
2. Place four slices of banana in each saucer.
3. Set each saucer on a sheet of paper. Label one of the papers "Without Vitamin C." Label the other paper "With Vitamin C."
4. Place the vitamin C tablets on the cutting board and crush them with the rolling pin.
5. Use the dinner knife to scoop up the vitamin C powder and sprinkle the powder over the cut surface of the banana slices in the With Vitamin C saucer.
6. Every 15 minutes for 2 hours or more, observe the color of each sample's surface. Record your observation in an Oxidation Data table like the one shown.

Results

The untreated banana slices slowly turn brown, but those covered with vitamin C are unchanged.

OXIDATION DATA

Time, minutes	Banana with Vitamin C	Banana without Vitamin C
15		
30		
45		
60		
75		
90		
105		
120		

Why?

Bananas discolor when bruised or peeled and exposed to air. This discoloration is caused by changes that occur when the cells are broken. The chemicals released by the damaged cells are **oxidized** (combined with oxygen), resulting in changes in the fruit. This process of change due to a combination with oxygen is called **oxidation.** Vitamin C is an **antioxidant,** a substance that inhibits (decreases or stops) oxidation. Covering the surface of the banana with Vitamin C inhibits the discoloration caused by oxidation.

FOR FURTHER INVESTIGATION

Lemons contain vitamin C. Would lemon juice stop the bananas from turning brown? A project question might be, How effective is lemon juice as an antioxidant?

Clues for Your Investigation

1. Repeat the investigation, adding a third test set of banana slices. Label the paper under the saucer "With Lemon Juice."
2. Use lemon juice squeezed from a fresh lemon.
3. Photographs of the banana slices at the start, periodically during the test, and at the end of the test can be displayed to represent the progression of any changes. The photographs also help to compare the effectiveness of the antioxidants.

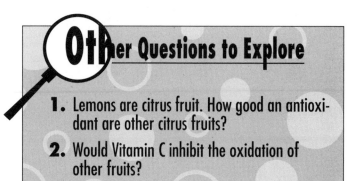

Other Questions to Explore

1. Lemons are citrus fruit. How good an antioxidant are other citrus fruits?
2. Would Vitamin C inhibit the oxidation of other fruits?

REFERENCES AND PROJECT BOOKS

Church, Jok. *You Can with Beakman: Science Stuff You Can Do.* Kansas City, Kans.: Andrews & McMeel, 1993.

Kenda, Margaret, and Phyllis S. Williams. *Science Wizardry for Kids.* Hauppauge, N.Y.: Barron's, 1992.

Strauss, Michael. *Where Puddles Go.* Portsmouth, N.H.: Heinemann, 1995.

VanCleave, Janice. *Janice VanCleave's Chemistry for Every Kid.* New York: Wiley, 1989.

Wollard, Kathy. *How Come?* New York: Workman, 1993.

Earth Science

31 Wet or Dry?

So You Want to Do a Project about **Humidity!**

LET'S EXPLORE

Purpose

To determine how water affects a pinecone.

Materials

large bowl
tap water
6 mature pinecones

Procedure

1. Fill the bowl with water, and place the pinecones in the water for 30 to 45 minutes.
2. Remove the pinecones and observe their scales.

Results

When the pinecones are soaked in water, they close up.

Why?

When the pinecones were soaked in water, their scales absorbed the water. The scales swelled and closed together.

water

FOR FURTHER INVESTIGATION

An instrument that measures **humidity** (the amount of moisture in the air) is called a **hygrometer.** Natural hygrometers are **hygroscopic,** which means they will absorb water from the air. Is a pinecone a natural hygrometer? A project question might be, How does humidity affect pinecone scales?

Clues for Your Investigation

1. Place three of the wet pinecones in a resealable plastic bag to keep them from drying out. With adult assistance, heat three of the six wet pinecones in an oven at low heat for 30 minutes or until the pinecones are dry. Ask an adult to remove the cones from the oven, using a heat mitten.

2. When the cones have cooled, observe the scales and compare them with the scales of the unheated wet cones.

3. For an extended project, tie a pinecone out-doors where you can observe it. Make daily observations for 2 or more weeks. Record the position of the scales and the humidity. The humidity can be obtained from the local weather report.

Other Questions to Explore

1. Are there other natural hygrometers?

2. How can humidity levels help predict the weather?

3. How would a pinecone hygrometer compare to a weather station's humidity instruments?

REFERENCES AND PROJECT BOOKS

Ardley, Neil. *The Science Book of Weather.* San Diego: Harcourt Brace Jovanovich, 1992.

Christian, Spencer. *Can It Really Rain Frogs?* New York: Wiley, 1997.

Cosgrove, Brian. *Weather.* New York: Dorling Kindersley, 1991.

Kahl, Jonathan D. *National Audubon Society First Field Guide: Weather.* New York: Scholastic, 1998.

Suzuki, David. *Looking at Weather.* New York: Wiley, 1991.

Time-Life Books. *Weather.* San Francisco: Time-Life Books, 1997.

VanCleave, Janice. *Janice VanCleave's A+ Projects in Earth Science.* New York: Wiley, 1999.

———. *Janice VanCleave's Earth Science for Every Kid.* New York: Wiley, 1991.

———. *Janice VanCleave's Weather.* New York: Wiley, 1995.

32 How Fast?

So You Want to Do a Project about the **Wind!**

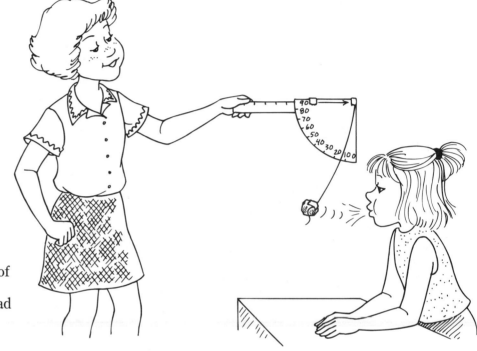

LET'S EXPLORE

Purpose

To measure wind speed.

Materials

drawing compass
6-inch (15-cm) -square piece
   of white poster board
scissors
protractor
marking pen
transparent tape
ruler
4-inch (10-cm) -square piece of
   aluminum foil
12-inch (30-cm) piece of thread
helper

Procedure

1. Use the compass to draw an arc connecting two diagonally opposite corners of the piece of poster board as shown.

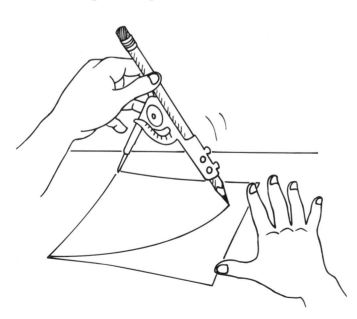

2. Cut along the curved line and keep the cone-shaped piece of paper. Discard the other piece.

3. Prepare a scale on the curved edge of the paper by using the protractor and marking pen to make marks 10° apart. Number the marks from 0° to 90° as shown.

4. At the 90° mark, draw an arrow across the straight edge of the paper. Tape this edge of the paper to the ruler.

5. Crumple the aluminum foil into a ball. Tape one end of the thread to the foil and the other end near the corner of the paper scale above the 0° mark as shown. The thread should hang so that when the ruler is held parallel to the ground, the thread hangs over the 0° mark on the scale. You have made a "windometer."

6. Hold the windometer so that the foil is about 12 inches (30 cm) in front of your helper's mouth. Ask your helper to blow toward the foil as hard as possible.
7. Observe where the string crosses the paper scale and record this number as a fast breeze in a Wind Speed Data table like the one shown.
8. Repeat steps 6 and 7 three times. Average the scale readings.
9. Repeat steps 6 to 8, asking your helper to blow gently on the foil.

WIND SPEED DATA

Wind Type	Windometer Scale Reading				
	Test 1	Test 2	Test 3	Test 4	Average
Fast Breeze					
Gentle Breeze					

Results

In a gentle breeze, the string moves slightly from its vertical position. A faster breeze causes the string to move farther up the scale.

Why?

Meteorologists (scientists who study the weather) use instruments called **anemometers** to measure the speed of wind. The "windometer" in this investigation is a type of anemometer. This instrument can be used to compare wind speeds but not to measure them. Moving air hits the foil and causes it to move. The speed of the wind hitting the foil is indicated by how far the ball moves, as determined by the position of the string across the paper scale. The higher the number, the faster the wind.

FOR FURTHER INVESTIGATION

Valleys between mountains and spaces between tall buildings act as a funnel to wind by directing or guiding the wind through these areas. Do funnels make the wind faster? A project question might be, How do natural wind funnels affect wind speed?

Clues for Your Investigation

1. Make a wind funnel by bending a 12-inch (30-cm) piece of poster board in half. Crease the fold, then open the paper slightly to form a V shape.
2. Repeat the original investigation, having your helper blow through the wind funnel at the foil just outside the funnel.

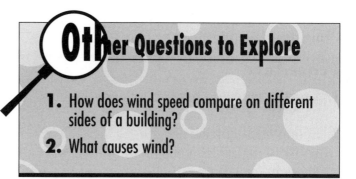

Other Questions to Explore

1. How does wind speed compare on different sides of a building?
2. What causes wind?

REFERENCES AND PROJECT BOOKS

Allaby, Michael. *How the Weather Works.* Pleasantville, N.Y.: Reader's Digest, 1995.

Campbell, Ann-Jeanette, and Ronald Rood. *The New York Public Library Incredible Earth.* New York: Wiley, 1996.

Christian, Spencer. *Can It Really Rain Frogs?* New York: Wiley, 1997.

Glover, David. *Flying and Floating.* New York: Kingfisher Books, 1993.

Lafferty, Peter. *Weather.* New York: Crescent Books, 1992.

Mandell, Muriel. *Simple Weather Experiments with Everyday Materials.* New York: Sterling, 1991.

Wood, Robert W. *Science for Kids: 39 Easy Meteorology Experiments.* Blue Ridge Summit, Pa.: Tab Books, 1991.

VanCleave, Janice. *Janice VanCleave's Weather.* New York: Wiley, 1995.

33 Fluffy

So You Want to Do a Project about **Snow!**

LET'S EXPLORE

Purpose

To determine the amount of air in snow.

Materials

masking tape
marker
four 10-ounce (300-mL) transparent plastic cups
snow
metric measuring cup

Procedure

1. Use the tape and marker to label the cups "A," "B," "C," and "D."
2. Scoop each cup across the surface of clean snow to fill it. Use your hand to level the snow in each cup, but take care not to pack the snow in the cups. Use fresh snow if possible.
3. Allow the cups to sit at room temperature until the snow melts.
4. Pour the water from cup A into the measuring cup. Measure the water in milliliters and record the volume of water in the melted snow in an Air Volume Data table like the one shown.
5. Repeat step 4 with cups B, C, and D.
6. Fill one of the cups to overflowing with water. Pour the water into the measuring cup. Read the measurement and record it in the data table as the volume of the cup. (The volume of the cup is equal to the total volume of snow and air that the cup can hold.)
7. Determine the volume of air in the snow by subtracting the volume of water in the melted snow from the volume of the cup. For example, if the volume of the cup is 300 mL and the volume of water in the melted snow is 80 mL, then:

$$300 \text{ mL} - 80 \text{ mL} = 220 \text{ mL}$$

The volume of air would be 220 mL.

Air Volume Data

Cup	Volume of Cup (total volume of snow and air)	Volume of Water in Melted Snow	Volume of Air in the Snow
A			
B			
C			
D			

Results

The cups full of snow melt, producing water that does not fill the cup. The amount of water will vary.

Why?

The more air that is mixed with the snow, the smaller the volume of water in the melted snow. When the snow melts, the air in the mixture is released.

Snow is composed of small crystals of frozen water called snow crystals. These crystals are formed when water vapor in the air condenses on a dust particle, forming a tiny water droplet. The water droplet is lifted high above the ground by rising air, where the temperature is below freezing, and the droplet freezes into a tiny ice crystal. If the temperature is around 5°F (–15°C) and there is plenty of water vapor, the ice crystal grows six branches and becomes a snow crystal. Snow crystals grow as water vapor freezes on them. The process by which a vapor changes directly to a solid without becoming a liquid is called **sublimation.** The shapes of the crystals vary, but they are all basically hexagonal (six-sided). The exact shape depends mainly on temperature.

Snowflakes are formed by the **accretion** (an increase in size by joining together) of snow crystals. As snow crystals fall through the clouds, they collide with other snow crystals, forming snowflakes. The size of a snowflake depends on the number of crystals in it. As the moisture content of the air increases, more snow crystals form, so more

of them will collide and form larger crystals. A 2-inch (5-cm) snowflake is considered very large. An 8-inch (20-cm) snowflake measured in Bratsk, Siberia, in 1971 was a megasnowflake.

For Further Investigation

As snow piles up, does it push on lower layers and squeeze out the air? A project question might be, How does the depth of snow affect its air content?

Clues for Your Investigation

Repeat the investigation with snow samples from different depths. Do this by removing a layer of snow with a shovel and scooping out the snow beneath. Take four or more samples from each different depth.

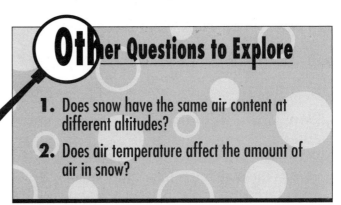

Other Questions to Explore

1. Does snow have the same air content at different altitudes?
2. Does air temperature affect the amount of air in snow?

References and Project Books

Ardley, Neil. *The Science Book of Weather.* San Diego: Harcourt Brace Jovanovich, 1992.

Christian, Spencer. *Can It Really Rain Frogs?* New York: Wiley, 1997.

Kahl, Jonathan D. *National Audubon Society First Field Guide: Weather.* New York: Scholastic, 1998.

Reader's Digest. *Why in the World?* Pleasantville, N.Y.: Reader's Digest, 1994.

Suzuki, David. *Looking at Weather.* New York: Wiley, 1991.

VanCleave, Janice. *Janice VanCleave's A+ Projects in Earth Science.* New York: Wiley, 1999.

———. *Janice VanCleave's Earth Science for Every Kid.* New York: Wiley, 1991.

———. *Janice VanCleave's Weather.* New York: Wiley, 1995.

34 Warmup

So You Want to Do a Project about **Temperature!**

LET'S EXPLORE

Purpose

To compare the rates of change of land and air temperatures.

Materials

2 outdoor thermometers
two 10-ounce (300-mL) plastic cups
light-colored soil

Procedure

1. Stand one thermometer in each glass.
2. Fill one of the cups with 1 inch (2.5 cm) of soil.
3. Leave the other cup alone. It is filled with air.
4. Allow the cups to stand at room temperature for 1 hour or until the soil and air are the same temperature.
5. Record the temperature of each thermometer as the starting temperature in a Temperature Data table like the one shown. Then place both cups in a freezer.
6. Every 10 minutes for 30 minutes, observe and record the temperature reading on each thermometer.

TEMPERATURE DATA

Material	Temperature, °F (°C)			
	Start	10 Minutes	20 Minutes	30 Minutes
Air				
Soil				

Results

The soil stays warmer than the air.

Why?

Temperature is a measure of how hot or cold a material is. A **thermometer** is an instrument used to determine temperature. For a material's temperature to decrease, it must lose heat. When the cups were first put in the freezer, the air in the cups was warmer than the air in the rest of the freezer. Since warm air is less **dense** (having parts closely packed together) than cold air, it rises and cold air sinks. Cold air quickly replaced the warm air in the cup. The soil, however, is denser than the cold air, so it doesn't move to allow cold air in. The soil in the cup loses heat slowly.

FOR FURTHER INVESTIGATION

Light-colored clothes absorb less heat than do dark-colored clothes. This is why you feel cooler when you wear light-colored clothes than when you wear dark-colored clothes. Do dark-colored things also lose heat more slowly than light-colored things? Would dark soil stay warmer longer than light soil? A project question might be, How does the color of soil affect its rate of temperature change?

Clues for Your Investigation

Repeat the experiment, determining the temperatures of different colored soil samples. You'll need a thermometer for each sample. Repeat the experiment four or more times for each sample and average the results.

Other Questions to Explore

1. How does land cover affect the rate of change of land temperature?

2. How does the rate of change of water temperature compare to that of air or land?

3. What causes land and sea breezes?

REFERENCES AND PROJECT BOOKS

Campbell, Ann-Jeanette, and Ronald Rood. *The New York Public Library Incredible Earth.* New York: Wiley, 1996.

Churchill, E. Richard. *365 Simple Science Experiments with Everyday Materials.* New York: Black Dog & Leventhal, 1997.

Gardner, Robert, and Eric Kemer. *Science Projects about Temperature and Heat.* Springfield, N.J.: Enslow, 1994.

Kenda, Margaret, and Phyllis S. Williams. *Science Wizardry for Kids.* Hauppauge, N.Y.: Barron's, 1992.

Potter, Jean. *Nature in a Nutshell for Kids.* New York: Wiley, 1995.

Soucie, Gary. *What's the Difference between Lenses and Prisms and Other Scientific Things?* New York: Wiley, 1995.

Strauss, Michael. *Where Puddles Go.* Portsmouth, N.H.: Heinemann, 1995.

Time-Life Books. *Planet Earth.* Alexandria, Va.: Time-Life Books, 1997.

VanCleave, Janice. *Janice VanCleave's Astronomy for Every Kid.* New York: Wiley, 1991.

———. *Janice VanCleave's Earth Science for Every Kid.* New York: Wiley, 1991.

Around and Around

35

So You Want to Do a Project about the **Water Cycle!**

LET'S EXPLORE

Purpose

To demonstrate the water cycle.

Materials

transparent storage box about the size of a
　　shoe box
ruler
sand
tap water
9-ounce (270-mL) plastic cup
plastic food wrap
ice cube
resealable plastic bag
medicine spoon (available at pharmacies and
　　used to measure accurate doses)

Procedure

1. Fill the box with 1 inch (2.5 cm) of sand.
2. Pour water into the box until the sand is thoroughly wet but doesn't have any water standing on its surface.
3. Set the cup in the center of the sand.
4. Cover the top of the box with plastic wrap.
5. Put the ice cube in the bag and seal the bag.
6. Place the bag in the center of the plastic wrap that covers the box.
7. Gently push the ice down about 1 inch (2.5 cm) so that the plastic wrap slopes down toward the center of the cup.
8. Set the box near a window so that the sunlight shines on the box.
9. Allow the box to sit undisturbed until the ice melts. This may take about 1 hour.

10. Remove the bag and tap the middle of the plastic wrap so that any water collected on its underside falls into the cup.
11. Remove the plastic wrap, then remove the cup.
12. Measure the amount of water collected by pouring it into the tube of the medicine spoon.

Results

Water droplets form on the underside of the plastic under the ice. Most of these water droplets fall into the cup.

Why?

The heat from the Sun provides energy, causing some of the water in the sand to evaporate and form water vapor. This water vapor then condenses on the underside of the plastic, which has been cooled by the ice. As more water collects on the plastic, the droplets increase in size until their weight causes them to fall into the cup below. The falling water drops represent rain. This is a model of the **water cycle** (the cycling of water between Earth and the atmosphere) on Earth. The sand represents the surface of Earth, and the plastic represents Earth's atmosphere. As long as the box remains closed, the amount of water in the box remains the same; it just moves from one place to another by changing from one form to another.

FOR FURTHER INVESTIGATION

Does it rain more over the ocean or the land? A project question might be, How does Earth's surface affect the water cycle?

Clues for Your Investigation

1. Repeat the investigation with boxes containing different surfaces. Replace the sand with different materials, such as moist soil, freshwater, and salt water. *NOTE: Ocean water is the equivalent of about 1 tablespoon (15 mL) of table salt per 1 quart (1 L) of tap water.*
2. Compare the amount of water in the glasses after the ice has melted.

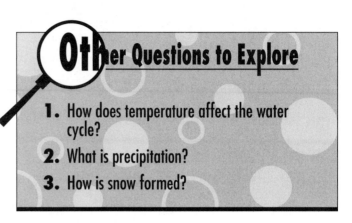

Other Questions to Explore

1. How does temperature affect the water cycle?
2. What is precipitation?
3. How is snow formed?

REFERENCES AND PROJECT BOOKS

Campbell, Ann-Jeanette, and Ronald Rood. *The New York Public Library Incredible Earth.* New York: Wiley, 1996.

Churchill, E. Richard. *365 Simple Science Experiments with Everyday Materials.* New York: Black Dog & Leventhal, 1997.

Mandell, Muriel. *Simple Weather Experiments with Everyday Materials.* New York: Sterling, 1991.

Suplee, Curt. *Everyday Science Explained.* Washington, D.C.: National Geographic Society, 1998.

Time-Life Books. *Planet Earth.* Alexandria, Va.: Time-Life Books, 1997.

VanCleave, Janice. *Janice VanCleave's Ecology for Every Kid.* New York: Wiley, 1966.

———. *Janice VanCleave's Oceans for Every Kid.* New York: Wiley, 1996.

———. *Janice VanCleave's Science around the Year.* New York: Wiley, 2000.

LET'S EXPLORE

Purpose

To determine the volume of air in soil.

Materials

    spoon
    4 cups (1 L) soil
    2 measuring cups marked in ounces and
        milliliters—one 2-cup (16-ounce, 480-mL),
        one 1-cup (8-ounce, 240-mL)
    tap water
    writing paper
    pencil

Procedure

1. Use the spoon to put 8 ounces (240 mL) of soil in the larger measuring cup. Do not press against the surface of the soil as you gently add the soil to the cup.
2. In the smaller measuring cup, put 8 ounces (240 mL) of tap water. Slowly add this water to the cup of soil. Record the starting volume of soil and water as 16 ounces (480 mL) in an Air Volume in Soil Data table like the one shown.
3. Allow the soil and water to stand 2 or more minutes. Then read the volume on the measuring cup and record this measurement as the final volume in the data table.
4. Subtract the final volume from the starting volume to determine the volume of air that was in each soil test sample. For example, the starting volume (the volume of soil by itself plus the volume of water by itself) is 16 ounces (480 mL) and if the final volume (the volume of soil and water together in the cup) is 12 ounces (360 mL), then the volume of air in the soil sample would be calculated as follows:

starting volume 16 ounces (480 mL) – final volume
12 ounces (360 mL) = 4 ounces (120 mL)

There are 4 ounces (120 mL) of air in the soil sample.
5. Discard the soil-and-water mixture, then clean and dry the measuring cup.
6. Repeat steps 1 to 5 three times.
7. Average the volume of air in the soil sample.

Results

The volume of water and soil combined is less than the starting volume of water plus soil.

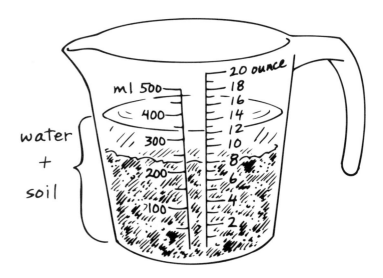

Air Volume in Soil Data

Soil Test Sample	Starting Volume Soil + Water, ounces (mL)	Final Volume Soil + Water, ounces (mL)	Volume of Air in Soil Sample, ounces (mL) (Starting Volume – Final Volume)
1	16 (480)		
2	16 (480)		
3	16 (480)		
4	16 (480)		
Average			

Why?

Soil particles are irregularly shaped, and as they stack together there is space between them that fills with air. When soil and water are combined, the air between the soil particles is **displaced** (pushed out of the way) by water. When you subtract the final volume from the starting volume of soil and water, you get the volume of air that was displaced.

For Further Investigation

Some soils have larger particles than others. The texture of soil depends on the size of its particles. A coarse-textured soil has large particles, and a smooth-textured soil has small particles. Is there more air in coarse or smooth soil? A project question might be, How does texture affect the amount of air in soil?

Clues for Your Investigation

1. Repeat the investigation with soils of different textures.
2. Display soil samples in plastic jars with lids.
3. Examine the soil samples with a magnifying lens and make drawings to compare the sizes and shapes of the particles.

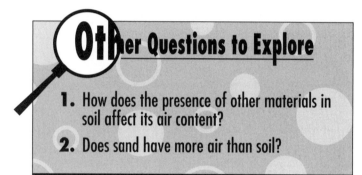

Other Questions to Explore

1. How does the presence of other materials in soil affect its air content?
2. Does sand have more air than soil?

References and Project Books

Campbell, Ann-Jeannette, and Ronald Rood. *The New York Public Library Incredible Earth.* New York: Wiley, 1996.

Farndon, John. *How the Earth Works.* Pleasantville, N.Y.: Reader's Digest, 1992.

Parsons, Alexandra. *Make It Work! Earth.* Ocala, Fl.: Action, 1992.

Potter, Jean. *Nature in a Nutshell for Kids.* New York: Wiley, 1995.

Redfern, Martin. *The Kingfisher Young People's Book of Planet Earth.* New York: Kingfisher Books, 1999.

Time-Life Books. *Planet Earth.* Alexandria, Va.: Time-Life Books, 1997.

VanCleave, Janice A. *Janice VanCleave's A+ Projects in Earth Science.* New York: Wiley, 1999.

37 Washout

So You Want to Do a Project about **Erosion!**

LET'S EXPLORE

Purpose

To determine erosion by water.

Materials

½ cup (125 mL) soil
four 12-ounce (360-mL) Styrofoam cups
tap water
spoon
cookie sheet
marker
pencil
2-cup (500-mL) measuring cup
helper
adult helper

Procedure

1. Pour the soil into one of the cups; dampen the soil with enough water to make thick mud, and stir.
2. With your hands, mold the mud into 8 equal size balls.
3. Place the mud balls on the cookie sheet.
4. Ask your adult helper to bake the mud balls in an oven at 275°F (135°C) for 1 hour or until they are dry.
5. Prepare the remaining three cups, to be called cups A, B, and C, as follows:

   - Use the marker to label the cups "A," "B," and "C."
   - Use the pencil to make 8 to 10 holes around the bottom edge of cup A. Place the mud balls in this cup.
   - Use the pencil to make 12 holes in the bottom of cup B.
   - Fill cup C with tap water.

6. Observe the shape of the mud balls in the cup.

7. Set the measuring cup on a table.
8. Hold cup A in one hand above the measuring cup and hold cup B just above cup A.
9. Ask a helper to pour the water from cup C into cup B.
10. After the water has drained out of cup A, observe the shape of the mud balls in the cup.

11. Allow the contents of the measuring cup to sit for 30 or more minutes. Then observe the amount of soil in the cup.

Results

The mud balls change shape. Parts of the balls are dissolved in the water, and parts are broken off. The dissolved and broken parts are washed out through the holes in the bottom of cup A, into the measuring cup. After a while, the soil settles to the bottom of the measuring cup. The amount of soil washed away varies depending on the type of soil used.

Why?

The mud balls are said to have eroded. **Erosion** is the process by which rock and other materials of Earth's **crust** (thin outer layer) are broken down and carried away by natural agents, such as water, wind, ice, and gravity. The part of the erosion process that involves only the breakdown of crustal materials is called **weathering.** One weathering process is **chemical weathering,** which affects the chemical properties of substances that make up crustal materials.

This experiment demonstrates one of the main causes of chemical weathering, the dissolving action of water. One part of the erosion process is the dissolving of some of the substances to form a solution. Another part is the mixing of the substances with water to form a **suspension** (a mixture in which tiny solid particles are spread throughout a fluid but are not dissolved and settle out slowly). The water erodes the mud balls by first dissolving and mixing with the substances in the ball, then carrying the substances away.

The agents of erosion in this experiment are water and gravity. Gravity pulls the water down, and the water carries the dissolved materials and mixed substances down with it as it flows out of the holes in the cup. When the water stops moving, gravity pulls the undissolved materials in the water down, where they collect in the bottom of the measuring cup. Particles of rock carried away by erosion are called **sediment.** The buildup of sediment is called **deposition.** Erosion is a wearing-down process and deposition is a building-up process.

FOR FURTHER INVESTIGATION

Earth's surface is made of different substances. Will rocky mud balls erode? A project question might be, How does the composition of a material affect its erosion?

Clues for Your Investigation

1. Repeat the original experiment with different mixtures of soil and aquarium rock. For example, mixtures might be one-fourth soil and three-fourths rock, half soil and half rock, or three-fourths soil and one-fourth rock.
2. For the most accurate results, mix enough mud so that each test can be repeated four or more times to compare the erosion of the different mud balls. Then average the results. Measure the soil collected in the cup to compare the rates of erosion of the different mud balls.

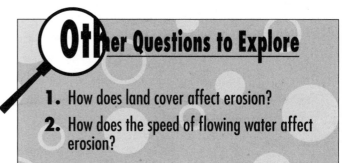

Other Questions to Explore

1. How does land cover affect erosion?
2. How does the speed of flowing water affect erosion?

REFERENCES AND PROJECT BOOKS

Campbell, Ann-Jeanette, and Ronald Rood. *The New York Public Library Incredible Earth.* New York: Wiley, 1996.

Churchill, E. Richard. *365 Simple Science Experiments with Everyday Materials.* New York: Black Dog & Leventhal, 1997.

Farndon, John. *How the Earth Works.* Pleasantville, N.Y.: Reader's Digest, 1992.

James, Ian. *Planet Earth.* Bath, England: Dempsey Parr, 1998.

Times-Life Books. *Planet Earth.* Alexandria, Va.: Time-Life Books, 1997.

VanCleave, Janice. *Janice VanCleave's A+ Projects in Earth Science.* New York: Wiley, 1999.

So You Want to Do a Project about **Settling Rate!**

LET'S EXPLORE

Purpose

To compare settling rates.

Materials

2-cup (500-mL) measuring cup
tap water
two 1-quart (1-L) plastic jars with lids
½ cup (125 mL) flour
½ cup (125 mL) dry red beans (Pinto
  beans work well.)
timer
helper

Procedure

1. Pour 2 cups (500 mL) of water into
   each jar.
2. Add the flour to one jar and the beans
   to the other jar.
3. Secure the lid on each jar.
4. Give your helper one of the jars, and you
   take the other one. You and your helper
   should start shaking the jars thoroughly
   when you say "go" and set them on the
   table after 30 seconds when you say "stop."
5. Observe and record the appearance of the
   contents of each jar in a Settling Rate Data
   table like the one shown. This will be
   recorded in the 0 minutes column.
6. Observe and record the appearance of
   each jar every 20 minutes for 1 hour. If the

beans and
water

flour and
water

flour and beans have not settled after 1
hour, continue to make observations once
an hour for 2 or more hours. (You may
wish to make your last observation after
the jars have stood overnight. Determine
the length of this time.)

Results

The beans mixed with the water as long as the
jar was being shaken, but settled as soon as
the jar was set down. Immediately after shaking, the jar of flour and water appeared cloudy.
Most of the flour settled within 20 minutes.
The time it takes for all the flour to settle will

SETTLING RATE DATA

Materials	Time						
	0 min.	20 min.	40 min.	1 hour	2 hours	3 hours	overnight, ? hours
Flour							
Beans							

vary, but for the author's experiment, it took about 3 hours for the water to start looking clear. However, even after sitting all night, there was still some flour floating on the surface of the water, and the water was not totally clear.

Why?

The shaking of the flour and beans in water represents different size rock particles being transported by fast-moving water. Placing the jars on the table represents the transport of the particles into a **stationary** (nonmoving) body of water. Rock particles or sediments, like the food particles in this experiment, are carried by swiftly moving bodies of water, such as streams and rivers, then deposited in stationary water, such as a lake. The time it takes a sediment to settle out of its transporting agent is called its **settling rate.** The settling rate of beans is much faster than that of flour. The flour represents **silt** (fine-grained sand). Since all the flour did not settle at the same time, this indicates that some flour particles are smaller than others. Larger particles of sediments settle out of water first, followed by progressively smaller particles.

FOR FURTHER INVESTIGATION

In a river, all the particles are mixed together. What kind of layers would be formed if several different size particles were put in the same jar? A project question might be, How does the settling rate of sediment affect horizontal layering in sedimentary rock?

Clues for Your Investigation

1. Repeat the investigation, using four jars and adding the flour, beans, and water together in each jar.
2. Photographs of the jars during the investigation can be displayed to represent the changes that occur.
3. You may wish to replace the flour and beans with soil, sand, and gravel (aquarium gravel can be used).

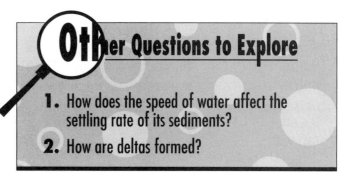

Other Questions to Explore

1. How does the speed of water affect the settling rate of its sediments?
2. How are deltas formed?

REFERENCES AND PROJECT BOOKS

Butterfield, Moira. *1,000 Facts about the Earth.* New York: Kingfisher Books, 1992.

Churchill, E. Richard. *365 Simple Science Experiments with Everyday Materials.* New York: Black Dog & Leventhal, 1997.

Redfern, Martin. *The Kingfisher Young People's Book of Planet Earth.* New York: Kingfisher Books, 1999.

Rillero, Peter. *Science Projects and Activities.* Lincolnwood, Ill.: Publications International, 1999.

VanCleave, Janice. *Janice VanCleave's Earth Science for Every Kid.* New York: Wiley, 1991.

———. *Janice VanCleave's A+ Projects in Earth Science.* New York: Wiley, 1999.

39 Squirter

So You Want to Do a Project about **Water Pressure!**

LET'S EXPLORE

Purpose

To determine a way to measure water pressure.

Materials

sharpened pencil
9-ounce (270-mL) paper cup
ruler
masking tape
2-quart (2-L) pitcher
tap water
2 metal spoons
helper

Procedure

1. Use the pencil to punch two holes of similar diameter in one side of the cup. Make one hole 3 inches (7.5 cm) from the bottom of the cup and the other hole 1 inch (2.5 cm) from the bottom and slightly to the left or right of the top hole.
2. Place a strip of masking tape over the holes on the outside of the cup.
3. Fill the cup and the pitcher with water.
4. Set the cup on the edge of a sink. Secure the cup to the counter with tape.
5. Remove the tape from over the holes in the cup, and ask your helper to keep the cup filled by pouring water from the pitcher into the cup.
6. Observe the distance each stream of water squirts out its hole in the cup.
7. Use the spoons to mark the spots where the water streams hit the bottom of the sink.

8. Use the ruler to measure the distance from each spoon to the side of the sink. These are the distances of the water streams. Record the distances in a Pressure Data table like the one shown.
9. Repeat steps 2 to 8 four or more times and average the distances. Record the averages in the data table.

PRESSURE DATA

Hole	Distance, inch (cm)				
	Trial 1	Trial 2	Trial 3	Trial 4	Average
Top					
Bottom					

Results

Streams of water squirt out the holes in the cup. The lower stream squirts farther.

Why?

Pressure is a force applied over an area. Since water has weight, it exerts pressure. One factor that affects the amount of pressure exerted by water is its depth. The pressure of water increases with depth because of the weight of the water pushing down from above. The greater the pressure, the farther the stream of water squirts, so the stream of water coming from the bottom hole squirts farther. In the ocean, the deeper you go, the greater the pressure of the water pushing down on you. For every 33 feet (10 m) you go down, the pressure increases by 15 pounds per square inch (1.1 kg per cm^2). In some of the deepest parts of the ocean, the pressure is as great as an elephant's weight pressing down on an area the size of a postage stamp.

FOR FURTHER INVESTIGATION

If the hole was bigger, would the stream go as far? A project question might be, How does the size of an opening in a water container affect the pressure of released water?

Clues for Your Investigation

1. Repeat the experiment, using three cups and making a different size hole in each—one large, one medium, and one small.

2. Take photographs of the water streams from the cups with different size holes and display them to illustrate your results. Diagrams of the squirting water with labels for the distance between the streams can also be used as part of a project display.

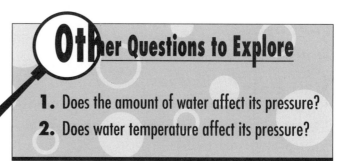

Other Questions to Explore

1. Does the amount of water affect its pressure?

2. Does water temperature affect its pressure?

REFERENCES AND PROJECT BOOKS

Ganeri, Anita. *The Usborne Book of Ocean Facts.* London: Usborne, 1990.

Glover, David. *Flying and Floating.* New York: Kingfisher Books, 1993.

National Wildlife Federation. *Ranger Rick's Naturescope Guides: Diving into Oceans.* Washington, D.C.: National Wildlife Federation, 1992.

Pernetta, John. *Atlas of the Oceans.* Chicago: Rand McNally, 1994.

Vecchione, Glen. *100 First-Prize Make-It-Yourself Science Fair Projects.* New York: Sterling, 1999.

VanCleave, Janice. *Janice VanCleave's Guide to the Best Science Fair Projects.* New York: Wiley, 1997.

———. *Janice VanCleave's Oceans for Every Kid.* New York: Wiley, 1996.

Walpole, Brenda. *175 Science Experiments to Amuse and Amaze Your Friends.* New York: Random House, 1988.

Wells, Susan. *The Illustrated World of Oceans.* New York: Simon & Schuster, 1991.

LET'S EXPLORE

Purpose

To determine the specific gravity of a rock.

Materials

scissors
ruler
2-L plastic soda bottle
one-hole paper punch
flexible drinking straw
2-cup (500-mL) measuring cup
pitcher
tap water
18-inch (45-cm) piece of string
apple-size rock
gram food scale
adult helper

Procedure

1. Ask an adult to cut about 4 inches (20 cm) off the top of the soda bottle. Keep the bottom and discard the top.
2. Use the paper punch to make a hole about 1 inch (2.5 cm) from the rim of the bottle.
3. Insert about ½ inch (1.25 cm) of the flexible end of the straw into the hole.
4. Bend the straw so that it forms a 90° angle. Place the measuring cup under the free end of the straw.
5. Use the pitcher to pour the water into the bottle until it is just above the straw. Water will flow through the straw and into the cup.
6. When the water stops flowing into the cup, empty the cup and then set the cup in place under the straw. The water-filled bottle and the empty cup are your specific gravity instruments.

7. Tie the string around the rock, then place the rock on the scale to determine as accurately as possible its mass in grams (g). Record the mass.

8. Holding the rock by the string, slowly lower it into the bottle.
9. When the water stops flowing into the measuring cup, record the amount of water in the cup in milliliters (mL). Use the following example to determine the specific gravity (S.G.) of your rock specimen.

   Example: A rock with a mass of 150 g displaces 60 mL of water.

   - specific gravity (S.G.) = mass of rock ÷ mass of water displaced by rock
   - mass of rock = 150 g
   - volume of displaced water = 60 mL
   - 1 mL of tap water has a mass of about 1 g, so the mass of displaced water = 60 g
   - S.G. = 150 g ÷ 60 g
     = 2.5

Results

The specific gravity of a rock is determined. For the example, the specific gravity is 2.5.

Why

Specific gravity (S.G.) is a physical characteristic used to identify rock types. Specific gravity is the ratio of the mass of a substance, such as a rock, to the mass of an equal volume of water. Your specific gravity instrument allows you to determine the volume of water that is equal to the volume of the rock. This is done by collecting the water displaced by the rock when placed in the instrument. Since the mass of 1 mL of water equals 1 g, the volume of water measured in milliliters is equal to the mass of water in grams. Specific gravity of the rock is calculated by dividing the measured mass of the rock by the calculated mass of water. Specific gravity tells you how many times more massive a material is than an equal volume of water. Most rocks have a specific gravity greater than 1, meaning that they are heavier than water.

FOR FURTHER INVESTIGATION

A larger rock would make more water pour out of the bottle. Does that mean a larger rock has a greater specific gravity? A project question might be, How does size affect the specific gravity of a substance?

Clues for Your Investigation

1. You will need different size samples of the same substance. Select rocks that look alike or pieces of a rock that has been broken. Rocks are made up of different **minerals** (naturally occurring substances that do not come from living things and have a definite chemical composition and a particular crystalline structure). If you have different size samples of a mineral, such as quartz, use them.

2. Repeat the investigation to measure and calculate the specific gravity of each sample.

3. Every substance has a certain specific gravity, so the specific gravity of a mineral or any substance can be a clue to its identity. If you determine the specific gravity of a mineral, compare the accuracy of your measurements to the known specific gravity of the mineral. You can find this information in a rock and mineral field guide.

Other Questions to Explore

1. What is the heft of a mineral?
2. What other physical characteristics are used to identify minerals?

REFERENCES AND PROJECT BOOKS

O'Donoghue, Michael. *Rocks and Minerals of the World.* San Diego: Thunder Bay Press, 1994.

Oliver, Ray. *Rocks and Fossils.* New York: Random House, 1993.

Pellant, Chris. *The Best Book of Fossils, Rocks, and Minerals.* New York: Kingfisher Books, 2000.

———. *Rocks and Minerals.* London: Dorling Kindersley, 1992.

Redfern, Martin. *The Kingfisher Young People's Book of Planet Earth.* New York: Kingfisher Books, 1999.

Ricciuti, Edward R., and Margaret W. Carruthers. *National Audubon Society First Field Guide: Rocks and Minerals.* New York: Scholastic, 1998.

VanCleave, Janice. *Janice VanCleave's A+ Projects in Earth Science.* New York: Wiley, 1999.

Zim, Herbert S. *Rocks and Minerals.* New York: Golden Press, 1957.

Physics

41 Equal

So You Want to Do a Project about **Potential Energy!**

Let's Explore

Purpose

To determine the effect of distance on the gravitational potential energy of an object.

Materials

1 cup (250 mL) dry rice
sock
gram food scale
calculator
meterstick
helper

Procedure

1. Pour the rice in the sock and tie the sock.
2. With the food scale, measure the mass of the sock to the nearest gram.
3. Determine the force weight (f_{wt}) of the rice-filled sock in the metric weight unit called **newtons** (N). Do this by using the calculator and the following equation. Record the weight as the force weight of trials 1 and 2 in an Energy Data table like the one shown.

$$\text{Force weight(N)} = \text{mass(g)} \times 0.0098 \text{ N/g}$$

4. Calculate the work (w) done if the sock was lifted a distance (d) of 0.5 m, using the following equation. The force needed to lift the sock is equal to its weight, which can be called the force weight (f_{wt}). Record the calculated work in the data table.

$$w = f_{wt} \times d$$

5. Ask your helper to hold the meterstick vertically with one end on the floor and raise the sock to a height of 0.5 m above the floor. Hold your hand just above the floor and in line with the sock.

6. Ask your helper to release the sock. Make note of how the sock feels when it hits your hand. Record your observations in the data table.
7. Repeat steps 4 to 6 using a height of 1 m.

ENERGY DATA

Trial	Force Weight (f_{wt}), N	Distance (d), m	Work (w), Nm	Observations
1		0.5		
2		1.0		

Results

The higher the sock is held, the more work that is done in lifting it and the harder it strikes your hand when dropped.

Why?

Energy is the ability to do **work,** which occurs when a force causes an object to be moved. **Potential energy** is stored energy. When an object is raised above a surface, it is said to have **gravitational potential energy.** The higher the object is raised, the greater its gravitational potential energy. Gravitational potential energy is also equal to the work done to raise it, which is equal to the work the object can do when it falls from its raised position.

As the object falls, its potential energy changes to kinetic energy (energy of a moving object). In this investigation, the sock gained gravitational potential energy when work was done on it by raising it. This stored energy changed to kinetic energy as the sock fell, and by the time it hit the hand, all the potential energy had changed to kinetic energy. The falling sock did work on the hand equal to the work that was done to raise the sock. The higher the sock, the greater the work done to lift it, the greater the amount of gravitational potential energy it has when it's at its height, and the greater the amount of kinetic energy it has when it hits the hand. Work and energy in this investigation are measured in Nm units, which are equal to **joules.** One joule is the amount of work done when a force of 1 N is applied over a distance of 1 m.

FOR FURTHER INVESTIGATION

A large rock would hurt more than a small rock if it fell on you. How would more rice in the sock affect its energy? A project question might be, How does mass affect the gravitational potential energy of an object?

Clues for Your Investigation

1. Repeat the investigation two or more times, using different amounts of rice in the sock each time but keeping the height the same for each test.
2. Record data in a table like the one shown.
3. Prepare a line graph comparing mass and work. Mass will be on the x-axis and work on the y-axis.

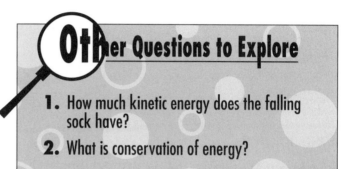

Other Questions to Explore

1. How much kinetic energy does the falling sock have?
2. What is conservation of energy?

REFERENCES AND PROJECT BOOKS

Ardley, Neil. *The Science Book of Gravity.* New York: Harcourt Brace Jovanovich, 1992.

Doherty, Paul, and Don Rathjen. *The Cool Hot Rod and Other Electrifying Experiments on Energy and Matter.* New York: Wiley, 1991.

Franklin, Sharon. *Power Up!* Glenview, Ill.: Good Year Books, 1995.

VanCleave, Janice. *Janice VanCleave's Gravity.* New York: Wiley, 1993

———. *Janice VanCleave's Physics for Every Kid.* New York: Wiley, 1991.

Wiese, Jim. *Roller Coaster Science.* New York: Wiley, 1994.

Williams, Brian. *Science and Technology.* New York: Kingfisher Books, 1993.

Wood, Robert W. *Mechanics Fundamentals: Funtastic Science Activities for Kids.* New York: Learning Triangle Press, 1997.

LET'S EXPLORE

Purpose

To observe diffraction of light.

Materials

straight pin
index card
pen
yardstick (meterstick)
desk lamp

Procedure

1. Use the pin to make a very small pinhole in the center and near the edge of one of the short ends of the index card.
2. Use the pen to draw a circle around the hole so that the hole is easy to find.
3. Fold the index card in half with the short ends together.
4. Partially unfold the card so that the two sides are perpendicular to each other.

5. Hold the card so that the end with the hole is in front of your face and the other end touches the tip of your nose.
6. Stand about 6 feet (1.8 m) or more from the desk lamp.
7. Close one eye and with the open eye look through the pinhole at the bulb of the desk lamp. What do you see inside the hole?

Results

You should see dark bands across the light in the hole.

Why?

Light is a form of energy that travels in **transverse waves** similar to water waves in shape. **Light waves** are disturbances that can travel through space in a regular pattern. Transverse waves have a **crest** (the highest point of a wave) and a **trough** (the lowest point of a wave). The distance from any point of one wave to the same point of the next wave is called **wavelength.**

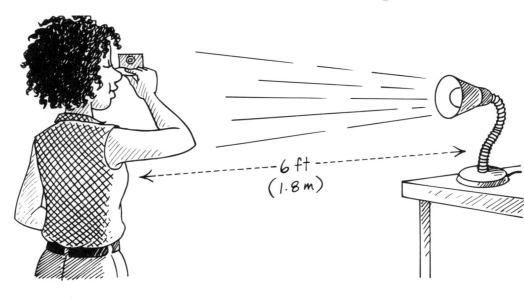

6 ft
(1.8 m)

When you look at the light through the hole in the index card, some of the light passing through the tiny hole spreads out instead of traveling straight ahead. This behavior of light is called **diffraction** (the change of direction of a ray of light around the edge of an object or through a small hole). The light that passes through the center of the hole goes straight, but light hitting the edge of the hole is reflected. Each point on the opening that reflects light acts as a source of light. When rays of light from different sources meet each other, they create bands of dark and light. This behavior of light is caused by the rays' wave shapes.

When two overlapping light waves meet and their crests and troughs match, the light energy adds together and the light is brighter. This is called **constructive interference.** But when the crests and troughs of the overlapping waves are opposite, the light energy is canceled, causing a dark area. This is called **destructive interference.** Despite the name, interference has no effect on the waves themselves, just on the way we see them. After meeting, the waves continue to move as they did before they met.

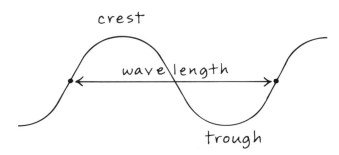

FOR FURTHER INVESTIGATION

When light from a distant star passes through the aperture of a telescope, the light is diffracted. Does the size of a telescope affect how it diffracts light? A project question might be, How does the aperture of a telescope affect light diffraction?

Clues for Your Investigation

1. Take the card from the original investigation and make several additional holes in it, each one a bit larger than the last, with the largest hole being about the size of a pencil point. Repeat the experiment, comparing the amount of interference in each hole. The clearer the light that passes through the hole, the less diffraction and hence the less interference.
2. From your results, determine which would produce more **resolved** (less blurred) images—a telescope with a large aperture or one with a small aperture.

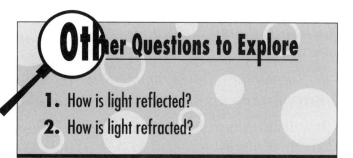

Other Questions to Explore

1. How is light reflected?
2. How is light refracted?

REFERENCES AND PROJECT BOOKS

Burnie, David. *Eyewitness Books: Light.* New York: Dorling Kindersley, 1999.

Gardner, Robert. *Science Projects about Light.* Springfield, N.J.: Enslow, 1994.

Glover, David. *Sound and Light.* New York: Kingfisher Books, 1993.

VanCleave, Janice. *Janice VanCleave's Physics for Every Kid.* New York: Wiley, 1991.

Wiese, Jim. *Roller Coaster Science.* New York: Wiley, 1994.

Williams, Brian. *Science and Technology.* New York: Kingfisher Books, 1993.

Wood, Robert W. *Light Fundamentals: Funtastic Science Activities for Kids.* New York: Learning Triangle Press, 1997.

43 Pickup!

So You Want to Do a Project about **Static Electricity!**

LET'S EXPLORE

Purpose

To demonstrate the effect of static electricity.

Materials

5 sheets of typing paper
one-hole paper punch
four 9-inch (23-cm) round balloons
marker
drawing compass
wool scarf
timer

Procedure

1. Inflate each balloon to about the size of a grapefruit and tie it. The balloons should all be the same size, and each should be easily held in one hand. With the marker, number the balloons 1 to 4.
2. Use the compass to draw a 6-inch (15-cm) -diameter circle in the center of each of the four remaining papers. Number the papers 1 to 4.
3. Fold one sheet of paper in half.
4. Use the paper punch to cut 26 circles from the folded papers.
5. Lay paper 1 on a table and spread the 26 cutouts within the circle drawn on the paper. Keep balloon 1 on the table and place the remaining papers, cutouts, and balloons away from the table so they will not be affected by steps 5 to 7.
6. Quickly rub balloon 1 back and forth across the wool scarf 10 times. Immediately hold the balloon near, but not touching, the cutouts for 5 seconds.

7. Count the number of cutouts that stick to the balloon. Record this number in a Static Electricity Data table like the one shown.
8. Discard paper 1, balloon 1, and the used cutouts.
9. Repeat steps 4 to 8 three times with the remaining materials.
10. Average the cutouts that cling to the balloons.

STATIC ELECTRICITY DATA

Balloon	Number of Cutouts Clinging to Balloon				
	Test 1	Test 2	Test 3	Test 4	Average
1					
2					
3					
4					

Results

Some of the cutouts leap up and cling to the balloon. The number of clinging cutouts will vary.

Why?

The smallest building blocks of matter are atoms, which in turn are made up of smaller particles. Atoms have a center, called a **nucleus,** which contains positively charged particles called **protons.** Spinning outside the positively charged nucleus are negatively charged particles called **electrons.** When materials are rubbed together, electrons tend to be rubbed off one of the materials and onto the other. This causes one of the materials to be more positively charged and the other more negatively charged. Energy due to the buildup of charges on an object is called **static electricity.** These charges are called **static charges** because they are stationary (nonmoving).

When two substances are rubbed together, such as the balloon and the wool scarf, electrons are lost from one substance and gained by the other. Rubbing the balloon causes it to collect negative charges. When the negatively charged balloon approaches the cutouts, the positive charges in the cutouts are attracted to the negative charges in the balloon. This attraction is great enough for the lightweight cutouts to move upward against the downward pull of gravity, and the cutouts stick to the balloon.

FOR FURTHER INVESTIGATION

Wool is a natural fiber. Would a fabric made from synthetic fibers generate static electricity? A project question might be, What effect, if any, do different fabrics have on the generation of static electricity?

Clues for Your Investigation

1. Repeat the investigation, using a fabric made from synthetic fibers, such as rayon or nylon.
2. Photos of the procedure can be used as part of your display.

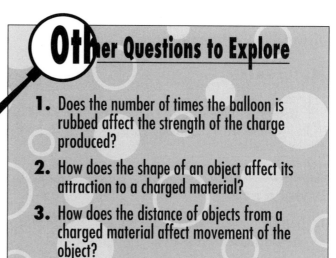

Other Questions to Explore

1. Does the number of times the balloon is rubbed affect the strength of the charge produced?
2. How does the shape of an object affect its attraction to a charged material?
3. How does the distance of objects from a charged material affect movement of the object?

REFERENCES AND PROJECT BOOKS

Ardley, Neil. *The Science Book of Electricity.* New York: Harcourt Brace Jovanovich, 1991.

Baker, Wendy. *Make It Work! Electricity.* New York: Scholastic, 1995.

Gardner, Robert. *Science Projects about Electricity and Magnets.* Springfield, N.J.: Enslow, 1994.

Glover, David. *Batteries, Bulbs, and Wires.* New York: Kingfisher Books, 1993.

Soucie, Gary. *What's the Difference between Lenses and Prisms and Other Scientific Things?* New York: Wiley, 1995.

VanCleave, Janice. *Janice VanCleave's Electricity.* New York: Wiley, 1994

———. *Janice VanCleave's Physics for Every Kid.* New York: Wiley, 1991.

Wood, Robert W. *Electricity and Magnetism Fundamentals: Funtastic Science Activities for Kids.* New York: Learning Triangle Press, 1997.

44 Swingers

So You Want to Do a Project about **Pendulums!**

Let's Explore

Purpose

To determine the frequency of a pendulum.

Materials

pencil
transparent tape
16-inch (40-cm) piece of string
metal washer
helper

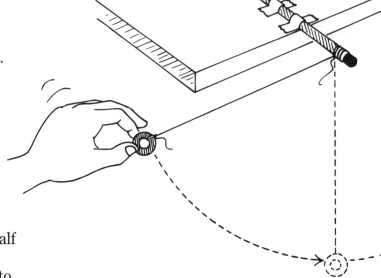

Procedure

1. Lay the pencil on a table so that about half the pencil extends over the edge of the table, eraser end out. Secure the pencil to the table with tape.
2. Tie one end of the string to the washer, and then tie the other end of the string around the free end of the pencil. You have made a pendulum.
3. Use your hand to lift the washer to one side so that it is level with the pencil and the string is straight.
4. Ask your helper to time 10 seconds. When your helper says "go," release the washer and let it fall. Count the number of swings (a swing is one complete back-and-forth motion) until your helper says "stop." If the final swing is three-fourths or more of a full swing, count it as one swing.
5. Record the number of swings in a Pendulum Data table like the one shown.
6. Repeat steps 3 to 5 three or more times. Average all the tests.

PENDULUM DATA

Number of Swings				
Test 1	Test 2	Test 3	Test 4	Average

Results

The author's pendulum averaged 9 swings.

Why?

The hanging string and washer is a pendulum. A **pendulum** is a weight hung by a rod or string from a fixed point in a way that allows the weight to swing back and forth freely. Every pendulum has a natural **frequency** (number of times a regularly repeating event, such as a pendulum moving back and forth, occurs per second) at which it swings when moved.

For Further Investigation

Would a longer string make the pendulum swing slower? A project question might be, Does the length of a pendulum affect its natural frequency?

Clues for Your Investigation

1. Prepare two more pendulums, one 10 inches (25 cm) and the other 24 inches (60 cm) long.
2. Repeat the original investigation, counting the swings of each pendulum in 10 seconds.

Other Questions to Explore

1. Does the weight of the pendulum affect its frequency?
2. Would a longer timing period affect a pendulum's frequency?
3. Does the height to which the pendulum is raised affect its frequency?

References and Project Books

Doherty, Paul, and Don Rathjen. *The Spinning Blackboard and Other Dynamic Experiments on Force and Motion.* New York: Wiley, 1996.

Franklin, Sharon, and Mary Leontovich. *Force, of Course!* Glenview, Ill.: Good Year Books, 1995.

Hann, Judith. *How Science Works.* Pleasantville, NY.: Reader's Digest, 1991.

Melton, Lisa Taylor, and Eric Landizinsky. *50 Nifty Science Experiments.* Chicago: Lowell House, 1992.

Potter, Jean. *Science in Seconds for Kids.* New York: Wiley, 1995.

VanCleave, Janice. *Janice VanCleave's Physics for Every Kid.* New York: Wiley, 1991.

———. *Janice VanCleave's 200 Gooey, Slippery, Slimy, Weird, and Fun Experiments.* New York: Wiley, 1993.

Wiese, Jim. *Roller Coaster Science.* New York: Wiley, 1994.

Wood, Robert W. *Mechanics Fundamentals: Funtastic Science Activities for Kids.* New York: Learning Triangle Press, 1997.

45 Spinners

So You Want to Do a Project about **Inertia!**

LET'S EXPLORE

Purpose

To demonstrate how inertia affects the motion of an object.

Materials

unshelled small raw egg
timer
helper

Procedure

CAUTION: After handling raw eggs, wash your hands and any materials touched by the eggs. Raw eggs can contain harmful bacteria.

1. Place the egg on a table. Once the egg is stationary, watch it for several seconds.
2. Give the egg a gentle spin and then release it. Observe its motion.
3. Spin the egg again and ask a helper to time the spin. When you say "go," your helper will start timing and you will start the egg spinning.

Record the time in a Raw Egg Spin Data table like the one shown.

4. Repeat step 4 three times. Make an effort to spin the egg with the same amount of force for each test. Average the spin times of the four tests.

RAW EGG SPIN DATA

Testing Material	Spin Time				
	Test 1	Test 2	Test 3	Test 4	Average
Raw Egg					

Results

The egg wobbles as it spins, then stops. The average spin time will vary.

Why?

The egg continues to spin after it is released because of inertia. **Inertia** is the resistance an object has to any change in motion. It is the tendency of a nonmoving object not to move and of a moving object to continue to move unless acted on by some outside force.

The material inside the shell of the raw egg affects the way the egg spins. When force is applied to the solid shell of the egg, the shell begins to move. But due to inertia, the liquid yolk and egg white inside do not start spinning as soon as the shell does. The force of the moving shell on the liquid inside causes the liquid to move, but slowly. The sluggishly moving liquid hits against the inside of the shell, causing the egg to wobble. The wobble reduces the spin time of the egg.

FOR FURTHER INVESTIGATION

Hard-boiled eggs are solid throughout. Would a hard-boiled egg spin longer than a raw egg? A project question might be, How does the phase of matter of an object affect its motion?

Clues for Your Investigation

1. Repeat the investigation with a hard-boiled egg.
2. To distinguish the eggs, mark an X on the hard-boiled egg.
3. A series of diagrams representing time-lapse photography of each egg with arrows representing the motion of the eggs can be used as part of your display. The diagrams placed side by side show when each egg stops spinning in relation to the other.

Other Questions to Explore

1. How does the force applied affect the spin time of the egg?
2. Does the size of the egg affect its motion?

REFERENCES AND PROJECT BOOKS

Ardley, Neil. *The Science Book of Motion.* New York: Harcourt Brace Jovanovich, 1992.

Churchill, E. Richard. *365 Simple Science Experiments with Everyday Materials.* New York: Black Dog & Leventhal, 1997.

Gardner, Robert. *Experiments with Motion.* Springfield, N.J.: Enslow, 1995.

Hann, Judith. *How Science Works.* Pleasantville, N.Y.: Reader's Digest, 1991.

Kerrod, Robin. *Book of Science.* New York: Simon & Schuster, 1991.

Potter, Jean. *Science in Seconds with Toys.* New York: Wiley, 1998.

VanCleave, Janice. *Janice VanCleave's Physics for Every Kid.* New York: Wiley, 1991.

Wood, Robert W. *Mechanics Fundamentals: Fantastic Science Activities for Kids.* New York: Learning Triangle Press, 1997.

46 Spacey

So You Want to Do a Project about **Matter!**

Let's Explore

Purpose

To demonstrate that matter takes up space.

Materials

nail
empty 16-ounce (480-mL) plastic soda bottle
　with cap
masking tape
tap water
empty soda can with pull tab
adult helper

Procedure

1. Ask an adult to use the nail to make a small hole in the side of the plastic bottle about 1 inch (2.5 cm) from the bottom.
2. Place a piece of tape over the hole in the bottle.
3. Fill the bottle with water and close it with the cap.
4. Stand the bottle on a counter next to a sink so that the hole in the bottle faces the sink.
5. Remove the tape from over the hole in the bottle and observe any flow of water out the hole.
6. Remove the cap from the bottle and again observe any flow of water out the hole.
7. Make sure the tab is completely pulled off the soda can, then fill the can with water.
8. Hold the can over the sink. Tilt the can and observe any flow of water out of the can.

Results

The water does not flow out of the bottle when the cap is on. The water does flow out of the bottle when the cap is taken off. The water also flows out of the opening in the can.

Why?

Water and air are fluids, which means they flow. Fluids are forms of matter. Because all matter takes up space, water cannot flow out of a bottle or can unless air flows in and takes its place. When the bottle was closed, no air could move into the bottle, so no water could leave. The water covering the hole in the bottle formed a skinlike film over the hole, which prevented the air from moving into the bottle. When the bottle was opened, air moved into the top and water moved out the hole. The hole in the open can is big enough to allow the liquid to flow out the bottom part of the hole while air is flowing in at the top of the hole.

For Further Investigation

Would a smaller hole let the soda out of the can? A project question might be, How does the size of the opening in a soda can affect its pouring ability?

Clues for Your Investigation

1. Repeat the experiment, using three empty soda cans of the same brand. Use tape and a marker to lable the cans "A," "B," and "C."

2. Use paper towels to dry the tops of cans B and C. Then use tape to cover one-third of the opening of can B and two-thirds of the opening of can C. Place the tape in the same direction across the two cans.

3. To compare the sizes of the openings in the cans, calculate the area of each opening. Cut a circle from graph paper to fit within the top ridge of the can. With a pencil, mark back and forth on the area of the paper that covers the opening in the can to make a pattern of the opening. Use a permanent marker to trace around the edge of the pattern. Count the squares on the paper within the outline. Whole squares or those that are more than half will each be counted as one square. Record this as the area of the opening.

4. To compare the amount of water that flows from each opening, tilt each can the same amount and measure the time it takes for all the water to pour out of the can. Test each can four times. Record the results in a Pouring Time Data table like the one shown. *NOTE: The number of squares for your can may differ from those shown in the sample table.*

5. Using the pouring time data, prepare a bar graph comparing the pouring times of the cans. Take photographs of the openings to use on a legend showing the area (number of squares) of each opening. You may wish to display photographs of the water being poured out of each can.

POURING TIME DATA

Area of Opening	Pouring Time				
	Test 1	Test 2	Test 3	Test 4	Average
A (9 squares)					
B (6 squares)					
C (3 squares)					

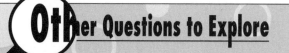

Other Questions to Explore

1. Would the direction of the opening in reference to the edge of the can affect the pouring time?

2. Are the sizes of the openings in cans of different brands of soda of uniform shape and size?

REFERENCES AND PROJECT BOOKS

Doherty, Paul, and Don Rathjen. *The Cool Hot Rod and Other Electrifying Experiments on Energy and Matter.* New York: Wiley, 1991.

Jones, Mary, and Geoff Jones. *Physics.* New York: Cambridge University Press, 1997.

Melton, Lisa Taylor, and Eric Landizinsky. *50 Nifty Science Experiments.* Chicago: Lowell House, 1992.

Nye, Bill. *Bill Nye the Science Guy's Big Blast of Science.* Reading, Mass.: Addison-Wesley, 1993.

Potter, Jean. *Science in Seconds with Toys.* New York: Wiley, 1998.

VanCleave, Janice. *Janice VanCleave's Physics for Every Kid.* New York: Wiley, 1991.

Williams, Brian. *Science and Technology.* New York: Kingfisher Books, 1993.

So You Want to Do a Project about **Insulators!**

LET'S EXPLORE

Purpose

To test the thermal conductivity of paper cups.

Materials

marker
four 10-ounce (300-mL) paper cups—two made for cold drinks, two made for hot drinks
3 ice cubes of equal size
saucer
timer

cold-drink cups   hot-drink cups

Procedure

1. Use the marker to label the cold-drink cups "A" and the hot-drink cups "B."
2. Put an ice cube inside an A cup and another ice cube inside a B cup. Put the remaining ice cube in the saucer.
3. Slip the second A cup inside the A cup with the ice cube so that the second cup rests on top of the ice cube. Repeat this step with the B cups.
4. After 5 minutes, look at the ice in the saucer. Then lift the top cup of each set to observe the ice cubes inside the closed cups. Continue making observations every 5 minutes until all the ice cubes completely

melt. Record your observations in a Melting Time Data table like the one shown. Use a check mark to indicate the presence of ice and an X to indicate the absence of ice. Determine the number of minutes it took for the ice in the saucer and the closed cups to melt.

Results

The ice cube in the saucer melts first, in the cold-drink cup second, and in the hot-drink cup last.

MELTING TIME DATA

Area of Opening	Melting Time, Minutes								
	5	10	15	20	25	30	35	40	45
Saucer									
A Cups									
B Cups									

Why?

Ice has a low **internal energy** (energy that indicates how hot or cold an object is). **Heat** is energy that flows from a material of high internal energy to a material of lower internal energy. The temperature of an object increases when heat flows into it and decreases when heat flows out of it. One type of heat transfer is called **conduction,** which occurs when molecules bump into each other, transferring heat from one molecule to the next. Heat is transferred faster through some materials and slower through others. **Thermal conductivity** is the measure of how fast heat flows through a material. The greater the thermal conductivity of a material, the faster heat flows through it.

Insulators like the hot-drink cups are materials that have low thermal conductivity, and **conductors** like the cold-drink cups are materials that have high thermal conductivity. In this investigation, you compared the thermal conductivity of two types of paper. The ice cube in the saucer was used as a control to determine if the cup materials affected the melting of the ice. Since the ice in the insulated paper cup took longer to melt, you can conclude that the insulated paper cup had lower thermal conductivity than the uninsulated paper cup. The paper in the hot-drink cup is a better insulator than is the paper in the cold-drink cup.

FOR FURTHER INVESTIGATION

The air in the closed cups was not able to move as freely as the air above the saucer. Is trapped air a good insulator? A project question might be, How does the motion of air affect its thermal conductivity?

Clues for Your Investigation

Repeat the investigation, adding a third set of cups made of Styrofoam. While paper may have some trapped air between the fibers, Styrofoam has a great deal of trapped air in it. Be sure the Styrofoam cups are the same size as the paper cups.

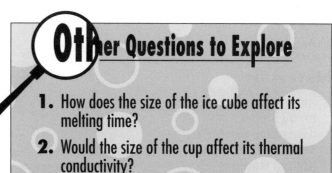

Other Questions to Explore

1. How does the size of the ice cube affect its melting time?
2. Would the size of the cup affect its thermal conductivity?
3. What materials have a high thermal conductivity?

REFERENCES AND PROJECT BOOKS

Doherty, Paul, and Don Rathjen. *The Cool Hot Rod and Other Electrifying Experiments on Energy and Matter.* New York: Wiley, 1991.

Franklin, Sharon. *Power Up!* Glenview, Ill.: Good Year Books, 1995.

Gardner, Robert, and Eric Kemer. *Science Projects about Temperature and Heat.* Springfield, N.J.: Enslow, 1994.

Jones, Mary, and Geoff Jones. *Physics.* New York: Cambridge University Press, 1997.

Nye, Bill. *Bill Nye the Science Guy's Big Blast of Science.* Reading, Mass.: Addison-Wesley, 1993.

VanCleave, Janice. *Janice VanCleave's Guide to the Best Science Fair Projects.* New York: Wiley, 1997.

———. *Janice VanCleave's Physics for Every Kid.* New York: Wiley, 1991.

Wollard, Kathy. *How Come?* New York: Workman, 1993.

Sliders

So You Want to Do a Project about **Heat!**

LET'S EXPLORE

Purpose

To determine how heat is transferred through a metal.

Materials

margarine
metal iced-tea spoon
3 identical plastic beads
1-pint (500-mL) jar
hot tap water
timer
adult helper

Procedure

1. Use as small a blob of margarine as possible to secure the plastic beads—A, B, and C—along the handle of the spoon as shown.
2. Ask your adult helper to fill the jar with hot water to a height just above where the bowl of the spoon will be.
3. Start timing as you place the bowl of the spoon in the water.
4. Observe the beads and record the time elapsed when each bead starts to slide in a Conduction Data table like the one shown.
5. Repeat steps 1 to 5 three times. Average the slide time for each bead.

Results

Some of each blob of margarine on the metal spoon melts and the margarine blob and attached bead slide down the spoon. The margarine under bead A melts first, and that under bead B melts next, followed by the margarine under bead C.

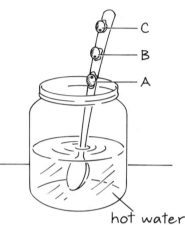

hot water

CONDUCTION DATA

Bead	Time				
	Test 1	Test 2	Test 3	Test 4	Average
A					
B					
C					

Why?

The hot water is a source of energy. The bowl of the spoon in the hot water **absorbs** (takes in) energy. As the molecules in the spoon's bowl move faster and faster, the temperature of the bowl increases. A substance may give up or absorb heat, but it does not contain heat. Energy is called heat only when it is transferred from one substance to another.

The faster-moving molecules in the spoon's bowl begin to collide with slower molecules in the handle. When they collide, the faster molecules transfer heat to the slower molecules, making them speed up. These molecules in turn collide with slower-moving molecules above them in the handle, exchanging heat. The transfer of heat by the collision of molecules is called conduction. Collisions of molecules and exchange of heat continue up the spoon's handle. As heat is transferred and the molecules speed up, the temperature of each part of the spoon increases. As the temperature of the spoon handle increases, heat is transferred to the margarine, melting it and allowing the beads to slide off. The bead nearest the hot water slides first, then the next bead up, then the bead farthest from the water (nearest the end of the handle).

For Further Investigation

As a rule, solids conduct heat better than liquids, and liquids better than gases. Which solids are the best heat conductors? A project question might be, Which material is the better heat conductor—metal, wood, or plastic?

Clues for Your Investigation

1. Air is a good insulator thus a poor conductor of heat, and wood and plastic have many air spaces. This might be a factor in the results.
2. Repeat the investigation with metal, wooden, and plastic spoons. Repeat the investigation four or more times and average the results. Try to use spoons with the same thickness of materials.
3. To make sure the water temperature is the same for each test, measure the tempera-

ture of the water, or use four or more samples of each type of test material and place them all in a large container of hot water at the same time.
4. Use equal size blobs of margarine as well as identical beads. Secure the beads at the same height from the bottom of the jar, regardless of the length of the spoon.
5. Record the time in a data table.

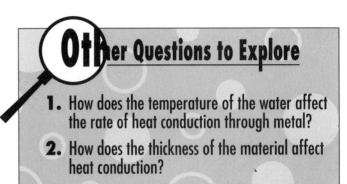

Other Questions to Explore

1. How does the temperature of the water affect the rate of heat conduction through metal?
2. How does the thickness of the material affect heat conduction?

References and Project Books

Gardner, Robert, and Erik Kemer. *Science Projects about Temperature and Heat.* Springfield, N.J.: Enslow, 1994.

Nye, Bill. *Bill Nye the Science Guy's Big Blast of Science.* Reading, Mass.: Addison-Wesley, 1993.

VanCleave, Janice. *Janice VanCleave's Guide to the Best Science Fair Projects.* New York: Wiley, 1997.

———. *Janice VanCleave's Physics for Every Kid.* New York: Wiley, 1991.

Williams, Brian. *Science and Technology.* New York: Kingfisher Books, 1993.

CONDUCTION DATA

Time	Metal Spoon					Wooden Spoon					Plastic Spoon				
	1	2	3	4	Average	1	2	3	4	Average	1	2	3	4	Average

49 Stretchy

So You Want to Do a Project about **Elasticity!**

LET'S EXPLORE

Purpose

To determine how elastic a gummi worm is.

Materials

rubber band
scissors
4 gummi worms
metric ruler

Procedure

1. From the rubber band, cut a section that is the same length as a gummi worm.
2. Place a gummi worm along the edge of a ruler. Measure the worm to the nearest 0.1 mm. Record this as the starting length in a Length Data table like the one shown.
3. Stretch the gummi worm as far as possible without breaking it, and record the greatest length as the stretched length.
4. Release the gummi worm, wait for it to stop contracting, and again measure its length. Record this as the final length.
5. Determine any change in length by finding the absolute difference between the starting and final lengths. This is done by subtracting the smaller value from the larger one.

LENGTH DATA

Materials	Starting Length	Stretch Length	Final Length	Change in Length
Gummi worm 1				
Gummi worm 2				
Gummi worm 3				
Gummi worm 4				
Rubber band				

6. Repeat steps 2 to 5 with the remaining gummi worms and the section of rubber band.

Results

The results vary. The author found the final length of the gummi worms to be slightly more than their starting lengths and the rubber band's final length to be the same as its starting length.

Why?

Elasticity is the ability of a material to return to its original shape after being stretched. A rubber band is generally considered perfectly elastic, meaning it returns to its original length after being stretched. The rubber band is used as the **standard** (a material against which other materials are compared) against which you are comparing the elasticity of the

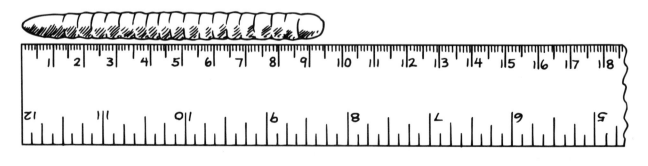

gummi worms. A gummi worm will generally contract to almost the same length at which it started. So the elasticity of the worm is great, but slightly less than that of the rubber band.

FOR FURTHER INVESTIGATION

When some metals are heated, such as gold, they can be stretched into thin threads, but they do not return to their original shape. Could gummi worms be stretched into a thin thread if heated? A project question might be, How does temperature affect the elasticity of a gummi worm?

Clues for Your Investigation

1. Repeat the investigation, changing the temperature of both the gummi worm and the rubber band. They can be heated by placing them in a plastic resealable bag and placing the bag in a bowl of warm water for a measured time. Cool them by placing the bag in a bowl of icy water, refrigerator, and/or freezer for a measured time.
2. Take photographs of the starting, stretched, and final gummi worms and rubber bands. Display the photographs along with samples of the gummi worms and rubber bands used.

Other Questions to Explore

1. What is the elastic limit of a material?
2. What happens if a material is stretched past its elastic limit?

REFERENCES AND PROJECT BOOKS

Bonnet, Robert L., and Dan Keen. *Science Fair Projects with Electricity and Electronics.* New York: Sterling, 1996.

Graf, Rudolf F. *Safe and Simple Electrical Experiments.* New York: Dover, 1964.

Hann, Judith. *How Science Works.* Pleasantville, N.Y.: Reader's Digest, 1991.

Jones, Mary, and Geoff Jones. *Physics.* New York: Cambridge University Press, 1997.

Murphy, Pat, Ellen Klages, and Linda Shore. *The Science Explorer.* New York: Owl Books, 1996.

Potter, Jean. *Science in Seconds for Kids.* New York: Wiley, 1995.

———. *Science in Seconds with Toys.* New York: Wiley, 1998.

VanCleave, Janice. *Janice VanCleave's A+ Projects in Chemistry.* New York: Wiley, 1993.

———. *Janice VanCleave's Molecules.* New York: Wiley, 1993.

50 High or Low?

So You Want to Do a Project about Sound!

LET'S EXPLORE

Purpose

To demonstrate the difference in pitch between open and closed wind instruments.

Materials

scissors
flexible drinking straw

Procedure

1. Make a cut through about three-fourths of the center of the flexible section of the straw. Do not cut the straw apart.
2. Bend the straw at the cut so that the two sections of the straw are at a 90° angle to each other. This is a model of a wind instrument.
3. Place the end of the shorter top section of straw in your mouth and cover the end of the longer bottom section with your index finger. Blow through the straw and listen to the sound produced.

4. Remove your finger from the bottom of the straw and blow again. Compare this sound to the first sound.

Results

The sound is higher when the bottom end of the straw is open.

Why?

Each section of the straw is a tube filled with a column of air. When you blow through the straw, the air inside moves forward, causing the air in the lower section to vibrate. Vibrations that travel through the air and other substances are called **sound.** Air vibrates faster in an open tube than in a closed tube. Since a faster vibration produces a higher **pitch** (highness or lowness of sound), open tubes have a higher pitch than do closed tubes. In wind instruments, such as the trumpet, clarinet, French horn, and pipe organ, vibrations in columns of air produce sounds with different pitches. If the instrument is closed—for example, by covering the flared-bell opening of a trumpet—a sound with a lower pitch is produced.

FOR FURTHER INVESTIGATION

Moving the slide on a trombone changes the sound produced. Is that because moving the slide changes the length of the tube? A project question might be, How does the length of the column of air in a wind instrument affect pitch?

Clues for Your Investigation

1. Fill a glass with tap water and set the glass near the edge of a table.

2. Repeat the investigation, holding the model wind instrument as before.
3. Place the end of the lower section just below the surface of the water in the glass.
4. Blow through the straw while you lower and raise the straw in the water. Listen to the sound produced as the straw is moved up and down in the water. From your results, determine how short and long columns of air affect the pitch of sound. You may wish to make a tape recording of the sound to be part of your display.

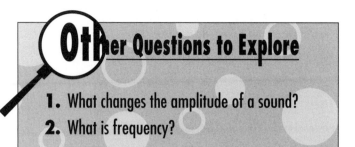

Other Questions to Explore

1. What changes the amplitude of a sound?
2. What is frequency?

REFERENCES AND PROJECT BOOKS

Ardley, Neil. *The Science Book of Sound.* New York: Harcourt Brace Jovanovich, 1991.

Franklin, Sharon. *Power Up!* Glenview, Ill.: Good Year Books, 1995.

Glover, David. *Sound and Light.* New York: Kingfisher Books, 1993.

Hann, Judith. *How Science Works.* Pleasantville, N.Y.: Reader's Digest, 1991.

Jones, Mary, and Geoff Jones. *Physics.* New York: Cambridge University Press, 1997.

Murphy, Pat, Ellen Klages, and Linda Shore. *The Science Explorer.* New York: Owl Books, 1996.

Potter, Jean. *Science in Seconds with Toys.* New York: Wiley, 1998.

Seller, Mick. *Sound, Noise, and Music.* New York: Shooting Star Press, 1992.

VanCleave, Janice. *Janice VanCleave's Physics for Every Kid.* New York: Wiley, 1991.

Wood, Robert W. *Sound Fundamentals: Funtastic Science Activities for Kids.* New York: Learning Triangle Press, 1997.

Glossary

absorb (1) To soak up, as liquid by a solid. (2) To take in, as energy by a material.

absorbency number A number that can be used to compare the absorbency of different materials, such as paper towels, as long as the same measuring instrument is used.

absorption The soaking up of a liquid by a solid.

accretion An increase in size by joining together.

adhesion The attraction between unlike molecules.

altitude Angular distance above the horizon.

anemometer An instrument used to measure wind speed.

angular distance The apparent or observed distance between distant objects, usually measured in degrees.

antioxidant A substance that inhibits (decreases or stops) oxidation.

aperture An opening in an optical instrument, such as the opening at the front of a telescope, through which light enters.

apparent size The size an object at a distance appears to be.

arc A segment of a circle.

atmosphere A blanket of gases surrounding a celestial body.

atom A building block of matter.

autumnal equinox The first day of autumn, on or about September 23 in the Northern Hemisphere.

axis An imaginary line that passes through the center of an object and around which the object rotates.

blade The large part of a leaf.

bond A force that links atoms together.

bonded Attached.

capillarity The tendency of liquids to rise or move through small tubes or openings of a porous material, such as paper.

celestial bodies Natural objects in the sky, such as stars, planets, moons, and suns.

cell The smallest building block of most living things.

cell membrane The thin outer skin of a cell that holds the cell together and allows materials to move into and out of the cell.

centripetal force The force on an object toward the center of its orbit.

cerebellum The part of the brain that controls muscle responses.

cerebrum The largest section of the brain, where all thought occurs and where input from nerves is interpreted.

chemical change See **chemical reaction.**

chemical reaction A process by which one or more substances are changed into one or more different substances. Also called a **chemical change.**

chemical weathering A type of weathering that affects the chemical properties of substances that make up crustal materials.

chromatography A method of separating parts of a mixture.

coalesce To join together.

cohesion The attraction between like molecules.

complemental air The volume of air that can be inhaled with force.

compound leaf A leaf in which the blade is divided into two or more leaflets.

concentration The amount of solute in a solvent, such as the amount of salt dissolved in water.

condensation The process by which a gas changes to a liquid.

conduction Heat transfer that occurs as a result of one molecule bumping into another one.

conductor A material that has high thermal conductivity.

conjunction The position of two celestial bodies where they are on the same celestial longitude line, one under the other but not one in front of the other, as seen from Earth.

constellation A group of stars that form a pattern in the sky.

constructive interference An effect that occurs when two overlapping waves meet and the crests and troughs of one wave match the crests and troughs of the other wave, as when light waves meet, causing the light energy to be added together and the light to be brighter.

contract To shorten or make smaller by drawing together.

control A test in which all of the variables in an experiment are the same except one.

crest The highest point of a wave.

cross-link A chemical bridge between two molecules.

crust   Earth's thin outer layer.

crystal   A solid that has its atoms arranged in a definite geometric shape.

cytoplasm   Technically, the entire region of a cell between the nucleus and the cell membrane.

dark adapted   Having a dilated eye pupil and hence increased light-gathering power of the eye.

debris   The remains of things that have been broken down.

dehydrate   To remove water from.

dense   Having parts closely packed together.

density   The mass per unit volume of a substance.

deposition   A buildup of sediment.

dermis   The inner layer of skin.

destructive interference   An effect that occurs when two overlapping waves meet and the crests and troughs of one wave are opposite the crests and troughs of the other wave, as when light waves meet and the light energy is canceled, causing darkness.

detergent   A chemical that cleans, especially if it removes oily dirt.

diffraction   The change of direction of a ray of light around the edge of an object or through a small hole.

diffuse   To spread freely.

digest   To break food into smaller parts.

dilate   To enlarge.

displace   To push out of the way.

dissolve   To break into small particles and mix thoroughly, as a solute dissolved in a solvent.

diurnal circle   The daily circular path of stars and other celestial bodies.

eclipse   (1) A celestial event that occurs when one celestial body passes in front of and blocks the light of another. (2) To pass in front of and block the light of.

ecliptic   The apparent path of the Sun across the sky.

elasticity   The ability of a material to return to its original shape after being stretched.

electron   A negatively charged particle spinning around the nucleus of an atom.

elliptical   Oval shaped.

emulsifier   An agent, such as detergent, that keeps one liquid suspended in small globules in another liquid, such as oil in water.

energy   The ability to do work.

epidermis   The outer layer of skin.

equator   An imaginary line that circles the center of Earth at latitude 0°.

equinox   The first day of spring or fall, occurring in the Northern Hemisphere on or about March 21 and September 23 and called **vernal equinox** and **autumnal equinox,** respectively.

erosion   The process by which rock and other materials of Earth's crust are broken down and carried away by natural agents, such as water, wind, ice, and gravity.

evaporation   The process by which a liquid changes to a gas.

exhale   Breathe out.

expiration   Breathing out.

fermentation   The process by which yeast digests sugar.

fingerprints   The patterns formed by the ridges of the fingertips.

fluid   A material that flows under pressure: liquid or gas.

freeze   To change from a liquid to a solid.

freezing point   The temperature at which a substance changes from a liquid to a solid.

frequency   The number of times a regularly repeating event, such as a pendulum moving back and forth, occurs per second.

friction   A force that opposes the motion of one object whose surface is in contact with another object.

fungus (plural **fungi**)   A plantlike organism that cannot produce its own food.

gas   A phase of matter that has no definite shape or volume.

geocentric   Earth-centered.

gravitational potential energy   Energy of an object that has been raised above a surface.

gravity   A force that pulls objects on or near the surface of Earth toward the center of Earth.

heat   Energy that flows from a material of high internal energy to a material of lower internal energy.

heliocentric   Sun-centered.

heterogeneous mixture   A combination of two or more substances that is not the same throughout.

hexagonal   Six-sided.

homogeneous mixture   A combination of two or more substances that is the same throughout; also called a **solution.**

horizon   An imaginary line where the sky seems to meet Earth.

humidity   The amount of moisture in the air.

hydrate   To add water to.

hydration The process by which water molecules surround a solute molecule; also called **solvation.**

hydrometer An instrument used to determine the specific gravity of a liquid.

hygrometer An instrument that measures humidity.

hygroscopic Absorbing water from the air.

hypertonic solution A solution that has a higher concentration of solute and a lower concentration of water than another solution.

hypotonic solution A solution that has a lower concentration of solute and a higher concentration of water than another solution.

impact crater A bowl-shaped depression caused by the impact of a solid body.

inertia The resistance an object has to any change in motion.

inferior conjunction The position of an inferior planet when it is between Earth and the Sun.

inferior planet A planet whose orbit is closer to the Sun than Earth's, namely, Mercury or Venus.

inspiration Breathing in.

insulator A material that has low thermal conductivity.

internal energy Energy that indicates how hot or cold an object is.

iron meteorite A meteorite that contains about 90 percent iron.

joule A unit of energy equal to the amount of work done when a force of 1 newton is applied over a distance of 1 m.

kinetic energy Energy of motion or of a moving object.

latitude Angular distance north or south of Earth's equator.

leaflet A single part of a compound leaf.

light A form of energy that travels in waves similar to water waves in shape.

light amplification The extent to which an object appears brighter when viewed through an optical instrument than with your unaided dark-adapted eye.

light-gathering power The measure of light amplification.

liquid A phase of matter that has no definite shape but has a definite volume.

liquid solution A solution made with a liquid solvent.

mass An amount of material.

matter On Earth, anything that has weight and volume; solids, liquids, and gases.

membrane A thin layer of animal or plant tissue.

meteor (1) A meteoroid that enters the atmosphere of a celestial body and becomes so hot due to friction with the atmosphere that it vaporizes and light energy is produced. (2) The streak of light produced by a meteor, commonly called a shooting star.

meteorite Any part of a meteoroid that reaches the surface of Earth.

meteoroids All the solid debris in our solar system orbiting the Sun.

meteorologists Scientists who study the weather.

microbes Are tiny living things visible only with a microscope, such as yeast.

mineral A naturally occurring substance that does not come from living things and has a definite chemical composition and a particular crystalline structure.

mitochondria (singular **mitochon-**

drion) The power stations of a cell, where food and oxygen react to produce the energy needed for the cell to work and live.

molecule A group of two or more atoms held together by bonds.

monomers Small single molecules connected in a polymer.

nerves Bundles of cells that send messages throughout the body.

netted venation A leaf vein pattern characterized by multiple branched veins, as found in leaves such as a sunflower or oak.

new moon The dark, unlighted phase of the Moon.

newton (N) A metric unit of weight.

non-Newtonion fluid A fluid that has some properties of a solid.

Northern Hemisphere The region of Earth north of the equator.

nucleus (plural **nuclei**) (1) A spherical or oval-shaped body, often in the center of a cell, that controls all cell activity. (2) The center of an atom.

orbit (1) The curved path of one body about another. (2) To move in such a path.

organelles Structures within a cell that have specific functions, such as the nucleus and mitochondria.

organism A living thing.

osmosis The movement of water through a semipermeable membrane.

oxidation The process of change due to a combination with oxygen.

oxidize To combine with oxygen.

palmately compound A compound leaf pattern characterized by several separate leaves that fan out from the petiole, as found in leaves such as those of a clover, horse chestnut, or poison ivy.

palmate venation A type of netted venation in which all the veins start at the petiole and extend through the blade like fingers on the palm of a hand.

parallel venation A leaf vein pattern characterized by large veins that are parallel with each other and the edge of the leaf, as found in leaves such as those of a lily or grass.

partial solar eclipse A solar eclipse that is visible to observers on Earth in the penumbra of the Moon's shadow.

pendulum A weight hung by a rod or string from a fixed point in a way that allows the weight to swing back and forth freely.

penumbra The lighter outer region of a shadow.

petiole The stalk of a leaf.

phases (1) Changes in the size and shape of the lighted side of a celestial body visible to observers on Earth. (2) Forms of matter: solid, liquid, and gas.

pigment A substance that gives a material color.

pinnately compound A compound leaf pattern characterized by leaflets attached along a central stalk, as found in leaves such as those of a rose, ash, walnut, or hickory.

pinnate venation A type of netted venation in which a single large vein runs through the center of the leaf and smaller veins branch from it in a feather shape.

pitch Highness or lowness of sound.

planet (from the Greek word for *wanderer*) A celestial body that orbits a sun and shines only by the light it reflects.

pliable Easily bent.

polymer A large, chainlike molecule made by combining many monomers.

potential energy Stored energy.

pressure A force applied over an area.

product A substance that a reactant changes into during a chemical reaction.

proton A positively charged particle in the nucleus of an atom.

reactant A substance that is changed during a chemical reaction.

reaction time The time it takes an organism to respond to a stimulus.

reflect To bounce back.

repel To push away.

reserve air The volume of air that can be forced out after normal expiration.

residual air The volume of air that always remains in the lungs.

resolved Less blurred.

revolve To move in a curved path around another object, as the Moon around Earth.

rotation The turning of an object about its axis.

salinity Salt concentration; amount of salt in water.

satellite A body that orbits a celestial body, including natural satellites such as moons orbing planets and man-made satellites such as weather satellites and spacecraft orbiting Earth.

sediment Particles of rock carried away by erosion.

semipermeable membrane A membrane that selectively allows materials to pass through.

sensory Having to do with sight, smell, hearing, taste, and/or touch.

settling rate The time it takes a sediment to settle out of its transporting agent.

silt A fine-grained sand.

simple leaf A leaf of a plant consisting of a single blade.

snowflake An accretion of snow crystals.

solar eclipse An eclipse in which the Moon passes directly between the Sun and Earth and the shadow of the Moon moves across Earth.

solar system A group of celestial bodies that orbits a star called a sun.

solid A phase of matter that has a definite shape and volume.

solute The substance in a solution that is dissolved.

solution A mixture of a solute and a solvent; also called a **homogeneous mixture.**

solvation See **hydration.**

solvent The substance in a solution that does the dissolving, such as water.

sound Vibrations that travel through air and other substances.

Southern Hemisphere The region of Earth south of the equator.

specific gravity (S.G.) The comparison of the density of a liquid or solid to the density of an equal volume of water; the ratio of the mass of a substance, such as a rock, to the mass of an equal volume of water.

spinnerets The silk-spinning organs of a spider, which are short, fingerlike structures located near the end of the underside of the spider's abdomen.

standard A material against which other materials are compared.

static charges Electric charges that are stationary.

static electricity Energy due to the buildup of charges on an object.

stationary Nonmoving.

stimulus (plural **stimuli**) Something that causes an organism to react.

stomata (singular **stoma**) Tiny openings in leaves through which gases can exit or enter.

stony meteorite A meteorite made of material similar to rock found on Earth's surface.

sublimation The process by which a gas changes to a solid, or a solid changes to a gas, without becoming a liquid.

superior conjunction The position of an inferior planet when it is on the opposite side of the Sun from Earth.

suspension A mixture in which tiny solid particles are spread throughout a fluid but are not dissolved and settle out slowly.

tangential Touching at a single point, as the forward motion on a satellite to its curved path.

taste buds Groups of sensory cells on the tongue and the roof and back of your mouth that are responsible for the sense of taste.

temperature A measure of how hot or cold a material is.

thermal conductivity A measure of how fast heat flows through a material.

thermometer An instrument used to determine temperature.

tidal air The volume of air involved during normal, relaxed inspiration and expiration.

total solar eclipse A solar eclipse that is visible to observers on Earth in the umbra of the Moon's shadow.

transpiration The process by which plants lose water through their leaves by evaporation.

transverse wave A wave with a crest and trough; light and water waves.

trough The lowest point of a wave.

turgor pressure The pressure inside a plant cell due to the presence of water.

umbra The dark inner region of a shadow.

universe Earth and all natural objects in space regarded as a whole.

vaporize To change to a gas.

variables Things that can have an effect on the results of an experiment, such as containers, light, and heat.

vein One of the long, branching, tubelike structures in a leaf.

venation The pattern of large veins in the blade of a leaf.

vernal equinox The first day of spring, on or about March 21 in the Northern Hemisphere.

vibration A back-and-forth motion.

viscous Thick; having a high resistance to flow.

viscosity Measure of thickness.

vital capacity The maximum volume of air that can be inhaled or exhaled during forced breathing.

volume An amount of occupied space.

wane To decrease in size.

water cycle The cycling of water between Earth and the atmosphere.

water vapor Water in gas form.

wave A disturbance that can travel through space in a regular pattern.

wavelength The distance from any point on one wave to the same point on the next wave.

waxing To grow in size.

weathering The part of the erosion process that involves only the breakdown of crustal materials. See also **chemical weathering.**

work A transfer of energy that occurs when a force causes an object to be moved.

yeast A one-celled fungus.

zenith (1) The point in the sky that is directly overhead. (2) The highest altitude of a celestial body above the horizon.

Index

absorb, 30, 107, 113
absorbency number, 55, 113
absorption, 54–55, 61
  definition of, 54, 113
  of heat, 76
accretion, 75, 113
adhesion, 54, 59, 113
altitude, 13, 113
anemometer, 73, 113
angular distance, 6–7
  definition of, 6, 113
  hand measurements, 7
antioxidant, 66, 113
aperture:
  affect on light diffraction, 95
  definition of, 20, 113
  of a telescope, 20, 95
apparent size, 11, 113
arc, 13, 113
atmosphere, 18, 113
atom, 49, 97, 113
autumnal equinox, 13, 113
axis, 8, 113

Barringer Meteorite Crater, 19
blade, 28, 113
Big Dipper:
  daily motion of, 8–9
  measurement of, 7, 8–9
bond, 49, 113
bonded, 49, 113

capillarity, 55, 113
celestial bodies, 5, 113
cell:
  definition of, 27, 113
  model of, 26–27
cell membrane, 27, 113
centripetal force, 14, 113
cerebellum, 41, 113
cerebrum, 41, 113

chemical change, 50–51
chemical reaction, 50–51
  definition of, 50, 113
chemical weathering, 83, 113
chromatography, 60–61
  definition of, 61, 113
coalesce, 65, 113
cohesion, 55, 59, 113
complemental air, 44, 113
compound leaf, 28, 113
concentration, 32, 113
condensation, 31, 113
conduction, 105, 106–107, 113
conductor, 105, 107, 113
conjunction, 16, 113
constellation, 6, 113
constructive interference, 95, 113
contract, 40, 113
control, 62, 113
Copernicus, Nicolaus, 5
crest, 94, 113
cross-link, 53, 113
crust, 83, 114
crystal:
  definition of, 49, 114
  ice, 75
  snow, 75
cytoplasm, 27, 114

dark adapted, 20, 114
debris, 18, 114
dehydrate, 39, 114
dense, 56, 114
density, 56, 114
deposition, 83, 114
dermis, 36, 114
destructive interference, 95, 114
detergent, 64, 114
diffraction:
  definition of, 95, 114
  of light, 94–95

diffuse, 48, 114
digest, 39, 114
dilate, 20, 114
displaced, 81, 88
  definition of, 81,114
dissolve, 33, 114
diurnal circle, 8, 114

eclipse, 10–11
  definition of, 11, 114
  partial solar, 11, 116
  solar, 11, 116
  total solar, 11, 117
ecliptic, 13, 114
elasticity, 108–109
  definition of, 108, 114
electron, 97, 114
elliptical, 11, 114
emulsifier, 64–65
  definition of, 64, 114
energy:
  definition of, 93, 114
  of light, 95
  kinetic, 106, 107
  internal, 105, 115
  potential energy, 92–93, 116
epidermis, 36, 114
equator, 13, 114
equinox, 13, 114
erosion, 82–83
  definition of, 83, 114
evaporation, 30, 114
evening star, 17
exhale, 44, 114
expiration, 45, 114

fermentation, 39114
fingerprints, 36–37
  definition of, 36, 114
fluid, 53, 114
freeze, 62, 114

freezing point, 62, 114
frequency, 98, 114
friction, 18, 114
fungi, 39, 114

Galileo, Galilei, 16
gas, 48, 114
geocentric:
    definition of, 4, 114
    model of, 4–5
gravitational potential energy,
    92–93, 114
gravity, 15, 114

heat, 106–107
    definition of, 105, 107, 114
heliocentric, 5, 114
heterogeneous mixture, 64, 114
hexagonal, 49, 114
homogeneous mixture, 58, 114
horizon, 6, 114
humidity, 70–71
    definition of, 70, 114
hydrate, 39, 114
hydration, 59, 115
hydrometer, 56–57
    definition of, 56, 115
hygrometer, 70, 115
hygroscopic, 70, 115
hypertonic solution, 33, 115
hypotonic solution, 33, 115

ice:
    melting of, 62–63
impact crater, 19, 115
inertia:
    affect on motion, 99–101
    definition of, 100, 115
inferior conjunction, 16, 115
inferior planet, 16, 115
inspiration, 45, 115
insulation, 104–105, 115
insulator, 105, 115
internal energy, 105, 115
iron meteorite, 19, 115

joule, 93, 115

kinetic energy, 50, 93, 115

latitude, 13, 115
leaflet, 28, 115
leaves:
    collection of, 28–29
    compound, 28, 113
    simple, 28, 116
light amplification, 20, 115
light-gathering power, 20–21, 115
liquid, 48, 115
liquid solution, 62, 115
lung, 44–45

mass, 48, 115
matter, 102–103
    definition of, 48, 115
    phases of, 48–49
measurements:
    angular, 6–7
    hand, 6–7
membrane:
    definition of, 32, 115
    semipermeable, 32, 116
meteor, 19, 115
meteorite:
    definition of, 19, 115
    models, 18–19
    size of, 19
    stony, 18, 116
meteoroids, 18, 115
meteorologists, 73, 115
microbes:
    definition of, 39, 115
    yeast, 38–39
mineral, 89, 115
mitochondria (singular mitochon-
    drion), 27, 115
molecule, 49, 115
monomers, 53, 115
moon, 22–23
    apparent size, 10–11
    new, 22, 115

phases of, 22–23
shadow of, 11
morning star, 17
motion:
    affect of inertia on, 100–101

nerves, 41, 115
netted venation, 28, 115
new moon, 22, 115
newton, 92, 115
Newton, Sir Isaac, 53
non-Newtonian fluid, 53, 115
Northern Hemisphere, 13, 115
North Star, 8, 9
nucleus (plural nuclei):
    of atoms, 97
    of cells, 27
    definition of, 27, 97, 115

orbit, 5, 14, 115
organelles, 27, 115
organism, 39, 115
osmosis, 32–33
    definition of, 32, 115
oxidation, 66–67
    definition of, 66, 115
oxidized, 66, 116

palmately compound, 29, 116
palmate venation, 28, 116
parallel venation, 28, 116
partial solar eclipse, 11, 116
pendulum, 98–99
    definition of, 98, 116
penumbra, 11, 116
petiole, 28, 116
phases:
    definition of, 16, 48, 116
    matter, 48–49
    Moon's, 22–23
    Venus's, 16–17
pigment, 60, 116
pinnately compound, 29, 116
pinnate venation, 29, 116
pitch, 110, 116

planet:
  definition of, 5, 116
pliable, 53, 116
polymer, 52–53
  definition of, 53, 116
potential energy, 92–93
  definition of, 93, 116
pressure, 86, 116
product, 50, 116
proton, 97, 116
Ptolemy, 5

reactant, 50, 116
reaction time, 40–41
  definition of, 40, 116
reflect, 22, 116
repel, 64, 116
reserve air, 45, 116
residual air, 45, 116
resolved, 95, 116
revolve, 5, 116
rocks:
  specific gravity of, 88–89
rotation, 8, 116

salinity, 57, 116
satellite:
  definition of, 14, 116
  orbit of, 14–15
sediment, 83, 116
  settling rate of, 84–85
semipermeable membrane, 32, 116
sensory, 4, 116
settling rate, 84–85
  definition of, 85, 116
shadow parts, 11
shooting star, 19
silt, 85, 116
simple leaf, 28, 116
sky measurements, 6–7
snow, 74–75
  crystals, 75
  snowflake, 75, 116
snowflake, 75, 116

soil, 80–81
  air in, 80–81
  temperature of, 76–77
solar eclipse, 11, 116
solar system
  definition of, 5, 116
  model of, 4–5
solid, 48, 116
solute, 32, 58, 116
solution, 58–59
  affect on freezing point, 62–63
  definition of, 32, 58, 116
  liquid, 62
solvation, 59, 116
solvent, 32, 58, 116
sound:
  definition of, 110, 116
  pitch of, 110–111
Southern Hemisphere, 13, 116
specific gravity, 56–57, 88–89
  definition of, 56, 89, 116
spiders, 34–35
spider webs, 34–35
spinnerets, 34, 117
standard, 108, 117
static charges, 97, 117
static electricity, 96–97
  definition of, 97, 117
stationary, 85, 117
stimulus, 40, 117
stomata (singular stoma), 30, 117
stony meteorite, 19, 117
sublimation, 75, 117
Sun:
  apparent size of, 10–11
  eclipse, 10–11
  shadows, 12–13
superior conjunction, 17, 117
suspension, 83, 117

tangential, 14, 117
taste, 42–43
taste buds, 42, 117
telescope, 20–21

temperature, 76–77
  change of, 105
  definition of, 76, 117
thermal conductivity, 105, 117
thermometer, 76, 117
tidal air, 45, 117
total solar eclipse, 11, 117
transpiration, 31, 117
transverse wave, 94, 117
trough, 94, 117
turgor pressure, 33, 117

umbra, 11, 117
universe:
  Copernicus's model of, 5
  definition of, 5, 117
  models of, 4–5
  Ptolemy's model of, 4–5

vaporize, 19, 117
variable, 31, 62, 117
vein, 28, 117
venation, 28, 117
  palmate, 28, 116
  parallel, 28, 116
  netted, 28, 115
vernal equinox, 13, 117
Venus, 16–17
  evening star, 17
  morning star, 17
  phases of, 16–17
vibration, 50, 117
viscous, 53, 117
viscosity, 65, 117
vital capacity, 44, 117
volume, 44, 117

wane, 17, 117
water cycle, 78–79
  definition of, 79, 117
water pressure, 86–87
water vapor, 30, 117
wave, 94, 117
wavelength, 94, 117

waxing, 17, 117
weathering:
  chemical, 83, 113
  definition of, 83, 117

wind, 72–73
  speed of, 72–73
work, 93, 117

yeast, 38–39
  definition of, 39, 117

zenith, 6, 117